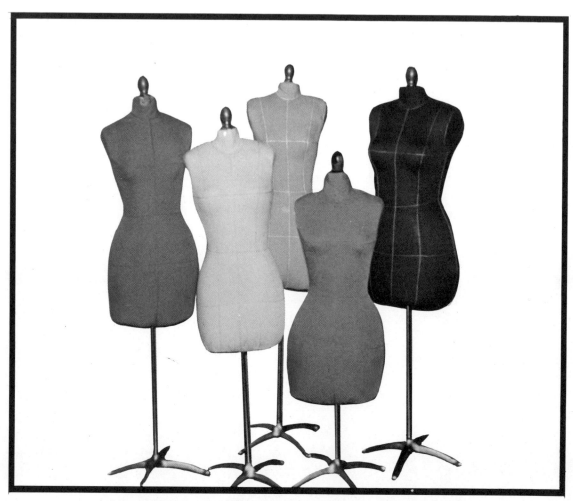

FIRMLY PADDED DRESS FORMS—PREREQUISITE TO ACCURATE DRAPING

design through draping

by

Martha Gene Shelden

Department of Home Economics
Fresno State College
Fresno, California

Illustrated by

RAY W. HELLBERG

Burgess Publishing Company

426 South Sixth Street • Minneapolis, Minn. 55415

Foreword

The Rockefeller Brothers' Report on *The Pursuit of Excellence* listed creative talent as one of our greates resources. (1)

Are we as teachers helping to develop this talent, or are we stifling it with standards of mediocrity?

Who are the creative among us? They are the ones who consciously build on ideas which come from the subconscious. Arnold states that they develop new solutions for old problems; they come up with unexpected couplings of ideas; they are able to meet a problem by figuring out an alternative plan. (2) Hass comments, "A creative individual has the power to visualize, to picture, to size things up for himself. " (3)

We should be developing creativity in the student - a talent perhaps lost since the days of his childhood. By encouraging the student to be creative, we are acquainting him with a satisfying means of use of leisure time -- one of the problems of the present and foreseen as an even greater one of the future. The creative individual needs a rich background and freedom to think, not regimented group activity or passive entertainment. Guilford reminds us that, "No doubt the more creative students are irritating at times and they are not ready to conform to the usual standards. " (4) Such a student is the one who often asks, "Why?"; he is the one who sees a short cut to class procedure.

Carl Rogers (5) in his paper "Toward a Theory of Creativity" says there is no fundamental difference in the creative process as it is evidenced in painting, in composing a musical number, in devising a new instrument, or in discovering a new procedure in human relationships. Let us as teachers, each in his own area of work, see what we can do to develop an atmosphere sympathetic to creativity. We need creative individuals today perhaps more than at any other time in our country's history.

Advanced clothing courses give the teachers an excellent opportunity to develop this permissive climate for creative work, to give the student an outlet for self-expression which he can carry into his mature life. This is one among many reasons for the organization of this text for draping -- to give the basic techniques, to advance to variations in basic designs, to give tools for developing original ideas, and finally, to inspire the student to express himself through his designs.

By using laboratory instructions which have been written, used, reworked, reused, and re-evaluated over a ten year period, these units have been written for an advanced college clothing class. A student needs a good understanding of and experience with commercial patterns before he attempts draping. Although flat pattern design is not required of the student, the author feels that the student advances better is she has studied flat pattern design before she begins draping.

The author has departed from the draping method and has used flat pattern in several places where experiences have taught her that the student accomplishes the task with a minimum of time and maximum of efficiency. These places are the set-in sleeve, the panel gusset, the shawl collar, and the preparation for draping collars.

No attempt has been made to include every type of variation. The ones which have been included, however, are planned to supply the needed stepping stones to more complicated designs which can be done independently.

The final unit "Designing for the Individual" is theoretical in contrast to the other units. It deals with the appeal of clothing and the reasons for this appeal; it reviews wardrobe planning, which the student has studied previously, but makes no attempt to develop the subject matter fully; and it presents suggestions for sources of designs.

May the student have a stimulating, creative experience with *Design Through Draping!*

REFERENCES

1. Sidney J. Parnes and Harold F. Harding, *A Source Book for Creative Thinking,* (New York, 1962).
2. *Ibid.,* 127
3. Glenn Hass and Wiles Kimball, *Reacting in Curriculum,* (Boston, 1965), 319.
4. Parnes and Harding, *op. cit.,* 165
5. *Ibid.,* p. 63

BIBLIOGRAPHY

Hass, Glenn and Wiles, Kimball, *Reacting in Curriculum,* (Boston: Allyn and Bacon, Inc., 1965). 319.

Parnes, Sidney J. and Harding, Harold F., *A Source Book for Creative Thinking* (New York: Charles Scribners and Sons, 1962).

Rogers, Carl, *Toward A Theory of Creativity*

Sikes, Geraldine B., *Creative Dramatics,* (New York: Harper Brothers Publishers, 1958).

Contents

Introduction

Design through draping is fun! It is a highly stimulating, creative expression! The reader may feel that she does not have the ability to be creative. Maslov believes creativity is a universal trait that most people lose as they grow up. However, it can be nurtured and, by degrees, be developed again. (1)

Each individual needs a creative activity because this type of experience is satisfying to him; it gives him inner exhilaration; he feels it is truly expressive of himself. It may be wholly mental or it may combine mental and physical. The product of one's creativity may not be new to society, but if it is drawn from the unconscious, it has the same value in achievement for the individual as something completely new to others. "And though our tiny efforts rightly pass almost unnoticed by the rest of mankind, they have a value for ourselves beyond what we can tell; one instant we have stood with the great ones of the earth and shared their glory. " (2)

Free time must be available for creativity, as it cannot be forced. Dorothy Lee thinks this should be unallocated and unscheduled time to produce something truly original and spontaneous. (3) In a school situation, free, unscheduled time is difficult to find; the application here is to try to find free time and, under any circumstances, to use the unconscious. Work on an idea, "sleep on it", don't force it - then, it is believed, an idea will come to the consciousness to be further developed; unconscious work followed by the conscious resulting in an unexpected coupling of ideas. (4)

There are unlimited types of creativity, and each type has its own rewards. In this writing the author will discuss creativity through dress design.

At an earlier time in the American culture, the home was a producing unit. The greater number of its needs were produced by the family. In the modern way of life, great specialization has developed. This results in most products being brought into the home in a completed form. Many of these purely utilitarian products can be produced more economically in industry than in the home. Some of them the homemaker would find, no doubt, rather boring to make. However, the fact must be recognized that although some things may have been monotonous to make, their preparation did give the homemaker a feeling of accomplishment. The modern woman still needs an opportunity for this feeling of achievement. If one searches, one finds that society offers many outlets for the desire to create. Few activities produce as great a sense of satisfaction as those which are manipulative and require self-discipline to accomplish them.

Meshke commented that the many attractions of modern life "...provide little if any inducement to self-discipline in the pursuance of time-consuming tasks. Consequently, the justification for clothing construction must be found within oneself at the intellectual level. Then conceived, clothing construction is a creative performance. Creative, not in response to necessity, but as an outlet for the human urge to explore, to experiment, and to discover. " (5)

Creative sewing is one of the most rewarding means of self expression. Home sewing for purely utilitarian purposes has been replaced in many American homes by the use of ready-made garments. However, for a woman to design and make a dress for herself or a member of her family can be highly satisfying. She may start with some detail - possibly the shape of the neckline - and let the idea grow from there. The skilled person should not choose designs and techniques which are repetitive of others she has completed but choose ones which challenge her creative ability. Constantly try something new (4) - then this can be a rewarding experience.

From the point of view of economy as well as creativity, it would be better use of both time and talent to make garments that would be high priced in ready-made clothing than to make simple garments which can be purchased inexpensively. The designing and construction of good garments by a skilled person is extremely profitable and an excellent means of extending the family income. In addition, the worker has the opportunity to develop a wardrobe in versions of the latest mode - expressing the individuality of the wearer, permitting her to select her own colors and fabrics, and adding the touch that makes the garment exclusively hers. The quality and charm of the products are limited only by the degree of creativity, the interpretation of personality, the skill of the worker, and the fabrics available.

Draping is a very rewarding way to accomplish creative designing. Draping is the manipulating of a fabric to obtain the desired design, effect, and feeling. In using this technique, the fabric "talks" to the worker, directs her work as she interprets the idea. Through this means she should obtain perfect harmony between the design, the fabric, and the figure of the wearer. One of the problems of many home dressmakers is the selection of the pattern in relation to the fabric. This inability to visualize the finished design correctly often results in much dissatisfaction and expense to the dressmaker. In draping one selects the fabric with a type of garment in mind and then works to get the desired effect by noticing the tendencies of the fabric to take on shape and form, and by giving careful attention to grainline. From this beginning the design develops.

Draping gives the opportunity to develop many kinds of designs. The idea is held by many that draping lends itself only to soft fabrics and dressy, often elaborate, designs. This is a mistaken impression. It is true that this type of garment can be developed easily through draping, but some women do not like to make this kind of frock nor care to wear it. However, the tailored garments which are not severe in line and are often described as being made by dressmaker tailoring are favorites with American women. They can be made charming and feminine through the addition of flattering details and softened lines and yet remain the simple garments which are very popular. The details and altered lines are valuable means of concealing an unfortunate bulge or of creating an optical illusion. Draping offers endless opportunities for expressing one's individuality.

The sketches in Figure 1 show dressy garments which lend themselves very naturally to draping. _A_ is made in a sheer fabric, probably chiffon, with much fullness introduced at the waistline. It uses the lining and the chiffon to give transparent and opaque contrasts for design effect. A pleasing combination of texture is seen in _b_ in which a sheer fabric is combined with lace in the skirt, around the midriff, and as edging on the scarf. The scallops of the bordered lace are used effectively in _c_ for the neck outline, for cuffs, and the yoke at top of the skirt.

Each of these garments shows great harmony of line, texture and design. In the draping of the fabrics, the designer undoubtedly let the fabric "talk to her."

Figure 2 shows garments which are basically simple in line but have softness added in construction lines inside the silhouette. In _a_ the dance frock has back interest through contrasting color in the panel which becomes full in the skirt area. Sketch _b_ has maintained trim lines throughout but added fullness in the skirt front. The peplum and inset above the waistline at center front give the design an added emphasis. Sketch _c_ has retained the simple lines in the blouse front and in the skirt back and front. Back interest is developed through the use of the deep cowl neckline and the slight fullness at the skirt top.

The clean-cut garments shown in Figure 3 demonstrate that the harshness of tailored lines can be softened by replacing the vertical, more masculine lines with diagonal and transitional lines.

As with all other media of expression, the fundamental techniques must be learned before one can make great progress. In the units that follow these techniques are presented. One method is given in detail for making a dress form; other methods are suggested. Instructions for variations for draping basic blouses and for simple skirts are given and then followed by other units presenting variations which may be copied or adapted to meet the needs of the selected design. The last unit presents topics to consider in designing for the individual.

After one has learned draping techniques, she may often combine several methods of designing. She may drape the whole garment but cut some part, perhaps a collar, from a favorite pattern. Possibly she may cut the skirt by a commercial pattern to insure capturing the silhouette of the season and drape the blouse. She may choose to cut the whole garment by her own basic pattern developed in flat pattern study but add her individual touch by some fabric manipulation of added feature or features. A fourth combination of methods can be the use of draping, flat pattern, and commercial pattern as these three complement each other for the experienced worker.

Whichever method or methods of designing the woman may choose, if she has let her unconscious work, has "listened to" the fabric, has applied her feeling of right and wrong in art, she should have created a garment which is truly hers.

REFERENCES

1. Sidney J. Parnes and Harold F. Harding, _A Source Book for Creative Thinking_, (New York, 1962), 95.

FIGURE 1 - SOFT, DRESSY FROCKS

FIGURE 2 - SOFT DETAILS ADDED TO TAILORED FROCKS

a

b

c

FIGURE 3 - TAILORED GARMENTS LEND THEMSELVES TO DRAPING

2. *Ibid.*, 119
3. Dorothy Lee, *Freedom and Culture*, (Englewood: 1959), 56.
4. Parnes and Harding, *op. cit.*, 129
5. Edna Meshke, *Textiles and Clothing Analysis and Synthesis*, (Minneapolis, 1961), 1-2

BIBLIOGRAPHY

Chambers, Helen G. and Moulton, Verna, *Clothing Selection*, (Chicago: J. B. Lippincott Company, 1961).

Erwin, Mabel and Kinchen, Lila, *Clothing for Moderns* (New York: Macmillan Company, 1964).

Hass, Glenn and Wiles, Kimball, *Readings in Curriculum*, (Boston: Allyn Becon Inc., 1965).

Lee, Dorothy, *Freedom and Culture*, (Edgewood Cliffs: Prentice-Hall, Inc., 1959).

Morton, Grace Margaret, *The Arts of Costume and Personal Appearance* (New York: John Wiley and Sons, 1964).

Meshke, Edna, *Textiles and Clothing Analysis and Synthesis* (Minneapolis: Burgess Publishing Company, 1961).

Oppenheim, Irene, *The Family As Consumers,* (New York: Macmillan Company, 1965).

Parnes, Sidney J. and Harding, Harold F., *A Source Book for Creative Thinking,* (New York: Charles Scribners and Sons, 1962).

Ryan, Mary Shaw, Clothing: A Study of Human Behavior, (New York: Holt-Rinehart-Winston, 1966).

Unit One
Making a Dress Form

A dress form is necessary for draping. It is valuable to the home dressmaker for fitting garments made by other methods as well. However, she must learn how to use it to derive the full value. There are several types of dress forms on the market. The completely adjustable ones are the least desirable because they do not reproduce the figure with sufficient accuracy. Adjustable ones which are covered with a fitted lining and padded to size are better. There are good foam dress forms available now, but they are expensive. (See Appendix A.)

A dress form that is a good reproduction of the figure can be made. Two methods will be given. The first method which is the more satisfactory is the use of a papier-maché form which is purchased in a smaller size than that of the individual and then padded to her exact contour and measurements. If the individual's waistline is very small, it is wise to order a form two sizes smaller. For tall girls the adjustable forms are recommended as the upper part of the torso can be raised, thus giving a longer length above the waistline. The advantages of the completed papier-maché dress form are: (1) it conforms to the individual's measurements; (2) it permits pinning fabrics into it in draping; (3) it stands firmly on its base; and (4) it can be repadded and recovered when the figure changes.

The papier-maché dress forms are made by several companies. (See Appendix A.)

The second method is to use adhesive tape over a T-shirt foundation while it is on the wearer; to slit vertically at center back to remove; to fasten together along the back slit; and to make or buy a wooden stand for it. When finished it can be covered with cotton jersey, thus giving something to pin to when draping. The advantages of this form are: (1) it is inexpensive; and (2) it conforms well to body shape. Many department stores carry kits which supply all materials needed to make this type of dress form. (See Appendix A.)

Supplies for Students

2 to 2 1/2 yards heavy muslin
 or heavy poplin in a chosen
 color for cover
wrist pin cushion
2 pounds bat cotton
milliner's glue (if desired)
5 yards muslin (80 sq.)
 for practice problems

white thread #50
heavy pins (office pins)
colored embroidery thread
 (heavy)
2 manilla folders - size 6
1 box pins with colored heads
1 box dressmaker pins
polyurethane foam

Two additional purchases may be advisable. If the individual is very tall, shoulder pads of foam rubber are helpful since the shoulder lines will be raised above that of the dress form. The adjustable dress form may also be used. A large bust can be padded more firmly if foam rubber "falsies" are used. An old brassiere of the type the individual usually wears can be used to give firmness and shape.

Supplies for Instructor

Princess line patterns in assorted sizes and reproduced in tagboard 14" x 24" squares (See Figure 5.)
tissue paper - 36" roll (can be purchased from a commercial pattern company)
cotton (Often a student will need a small amount in addition to her purchase.)

Measurements

Accurate measurements must be taken, if the muslin is to be the correct size, and if the final measurements of the dress form are to correspond with the figure. Measurements must be taken over the brassiere, the girdle, the panties and the slip. For each fitting the brassiere used should be freshly washed and of the style usually worn.

Use chart in Table 1 and take measurements as shown in Figure 4. It is more convenient to work in groups of 3 for the measuring.

Preparation of the Pattern and Cutting of a Muslin Shell

Use a pattern that is designed on the French dart lines, which are also called princess lines. A true princess line dress is cut with seams on the French dart line, which run, in front, from the center of the shoulder line to the tip of the breast, to the waistline, to the lower end of the skirt dart, and then to the bottom of the skirt. In back, the line extends from the midpoint of the shoulder seam, to the tip of the shoulder blade, to the vertical darts, the waistline, to the lower end of the skirt dart, and continues on into the skirt. (See Figure 6.)

It will need both center front and center back seams. When completed it must fit smoothly with no ease.

The size of the commercial pattern usually used will be too large because of the ease allowed for outer garments. The pattern the next size smaller may be the best choice, although it will probably be too large in the bust if the individual is of average measurements for her size. It will need to be taken up in fitting, if it is too large.

Five measurements from the chart above will be used to check the pattern size, namely: circumference measurements at (1) bust, (2) waistline, (3) hips 7" below waistline, (4) hips at largest part, and (5) blouse at center

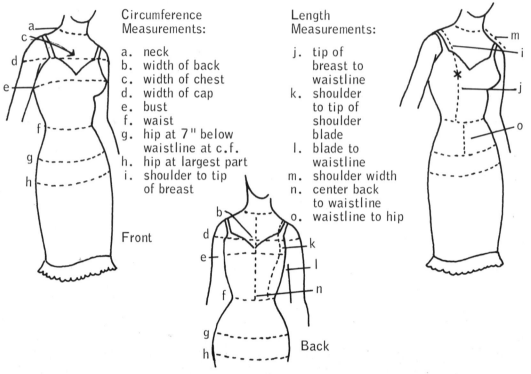

Circumference
Measurements:

a. neck
b. width of back
c. width of chest
d. width of cap
e. bust
f. waist
g. hip at 7" below
   waistline at c.f.
h. hip at largest part
i. shoulder to tip
   of breast

Length
Measurements:

j. tip of
   breast to
   waistline
k. shoulder
   to tip of
   shoulder
   blade
l. blade to
   waistline
m. shoulder width
n. center back
   to waistline
o. waistline to hip

Front

Back

FIGURE 4 - LOCATION OF NEEDED MEASUREMENTS

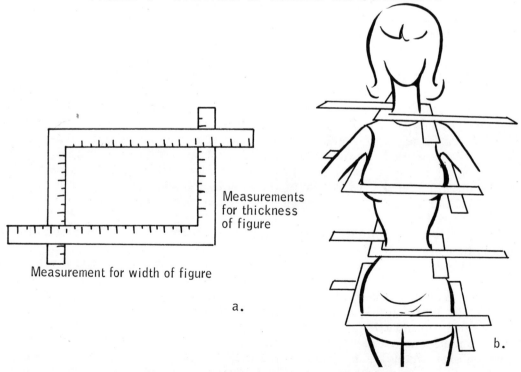

Measurements
for thickness
of figure

Measurement for width of figure

a.

b.

FIGURE 5 - MEASUREMENTS WITH SQUARE

TABLE 1 - MEASUREMENT CHART

Circumference Measurements		
neck	12 1/2"	No
width of back (4" below thoracic vertebra) ?	[illegible]"	✓
width of chest	12	✓
width of cap (extension of two above)	Front 19 1/2	Back 21
bust	36	✓
waist	28	✓
hip	37 1/2	✓
7" down from waistline	38 1/2	✓
__"below waistline (largest part of hips)		

Length Measurements in Blouse Area	Left	Right	
center shoulder to tip of breast	10	10	✓
tip of breast to waistline	6 3/4	6 3/4	✓
center back shoulder to tip of shoulder blades	7	8	✓
tip of shoulder blades to waistline	8	8 1/4	✓
underarm (at base of pit) to waistline	9	9 1/4	?
shoulder width (from base of neck end of shoulder)	6	5 3/4	No
center back to waistline	15 3/4		✓

Length Measurements in Skirt Area			
waistline to 7" hipline (at center front) c.f. 7 c.b. 6 3/4 sides. Left 6 1/2 Right 6 1/2			✓
measurements from waistline to location under buttocks (lean over to take measurement)	11 1/2	11 1/2	✓

Measurements with Squares (See Figure 5)	Thickness	Width
hip	9 3/4	13/8
bust	8 1/4	11 1/4
waistline	6 1/2	9 1/2
front and back neck	4 1/4	4 1/4

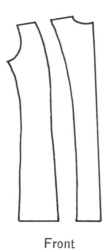
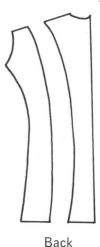

Front   Back

FIGURE 6 - BASIC PATTERN WITH PRINCESS LINES

back. (The other measurements in Table 1 will be used when working on the dress form.)

Compare these five measurements on the pattern by placing the pieces in their related positions. Compare the chart measurements with those of the pattern to determine whether alterations are needed to increase, decrease, or whether there are no changes to make.

Proceed with the pattern and the muslin shell as follows:
1. Make all the alterations on the pattern.
2. Allow 1" seam allowances in all areas except at neck, armholes, center front, and French dartline. Allow 5/8" on all other seams.
3. Place center back along selvage with 1" seam allowance.
4. Measure length to come up under the buttocks. In addition allow for a 1 1/4" casting at lower edge and an extra length 6" to 10" for length of dress form.
5. Straighten the muslin.
6. Pin the pattern on the muslin, and cut out the shell.
7. Mark the notches and darts.

Making the Muslin Shell

When the cutting is completed, staystitch around the neck, the armholes, and on the seamline down center back. (See the staystitching chart on page 27.) The stitching at center back is to give added strength where there will be strain in fitting on the dressform. Machine baste all seams except at the shoulders and the center front seam above the waistline. Hand baste the latter ones. Turn the seam allowance under on the left side of center back; press it. Place matching crossmarkings on the right and left sides as guides along the back seam to pin for fitting. Place these markings 4" below the neckline, at the waistline, 4" below the waistline and 8" below. (See Figure 7.)

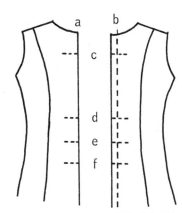

a. folded edge
b. machine stitching marking
   center back
c. stitching 4" below neckline
d. stitching at waistline
e. stitching 4" below waistline
f. stitching 8" below waistline

FIGURE 7 - LOCATION OF CROSSMARKINGS AT CENTER BACK

Fitting

Put the garment on right side out (over bra, slip, panties, and girdle). Pin the center back seam first on the crossmarkings and then at points in between them. Pin in the darts running from the center front toward the tip of the breast and from the armhole toward the tip of breast. (See Figure 8.) These darts should define each breast separately. On a full bustline two darts running each way from the center seam may be needed. The dart running diagonally from the armhole toward the tip of the breast is needed to make the dress form conform with the body hollow. (See Figure 8.) On an individual who has a very hollow chest additional darts may be needed to give the proper contour. A dart running from the armhole toward the shoulder blades may be needed on each side in the back to reproduce the curve of the shoulder. (See Figure 8.) The armseye (armhole) should fit snugly.

The center front and the center back seams must remain true throughout the fittings. No changes are made on them. In other words, they remain straight lines. The side seam should run in a straight line from the middle of the pit under the arm straight down to the middle of the ankle. It should be at right angles to the floor. The dress form should mold the thighs and the buttocks. Darts will be needed, both back and front, to accomplish this, and the seam curved in below the largest part of the hip and on the thigh.

Fit the shoulder seam so that it runs down the crest of the shoulder. Clip the neck to the staystitching, if needed to make the seam lie smoothly. The staystitching around the neck should outline the base of the neck. If it does not, relocate it by pencil markings.

Remove the muslin shell and hand baste all the darts which have been added and all the alterations on the side seams, shoulder, and French dart line seams. Make a new staystitching line at the neck, if needed.

Refit the muslin shell to check the new darts and seam lines. Make any further alterations needed to produce a smoothly fitted garment. Complete the alterations and refit. Repeat altering and refitting as often as necessary.

Place a rubber band around each arm at shoulder to show the location of the armseye for each arm. Mark with pencil the new staystitching line, if the first does not follow this pencil line. Check the length of the shoulder with the measurement on Table 1.

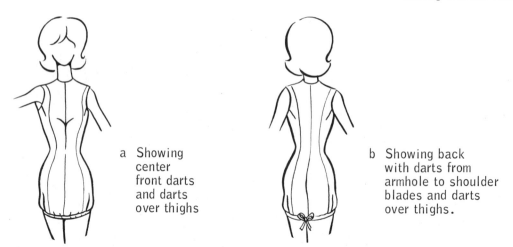

a Showing
center
front darts
and darts
over thighs

b Showing back
with darts from
armhole to shoulder
blades and darts
over thighs.

FIGURE 8 - FITTED MUSLIN SHELL

The muslin shell must be long enough to pull under the lower edge of the dress form with enough length to turn under 1 1/4" to make a casing through which a tape can run. If the shell has been cut too short, a casing can be made of an extra piece of muslin and sewed around the bottom.

At the last fitting, place tape measures around the figure at bustline, waistline, and hipline. Pin them to slip to keep in place. These must parallel the floor. Mark lightly with pencil along the lower edge of the tape measure in these three locations. These markings will be used for the lines of couching as instructed below.

The seams are now ready for permanent stitching. Because of the stretch in the muslin during padding, stitch each seam 1/16" to the inside of the basting, thus making the shell smaller. This stretch has been caused by pulling the fabric repeatedly during padding. Trim all the seams, except at center back, to 1/2". Clip the concave curves. Press the muslin shell with a dry iron, and take great care to not stretch the fabric by pressing off-grain.

Mark, with colored embroidery thread, the bust, hip, and waistlines either with couching by machine or hand. This will mark the important lines so that they can be located by your fingers under the material as you drape. Make the hem or casing 1 1/4" wide at bottom. Make a pull for this casing by tearing a strip 2 1/2" wide along the selvage. Press the raw edge under 1/4", fold the strip in half lengthwise so the folded edge lies on the selvage edge; stitch along the folded edges. (See Figure 9.)

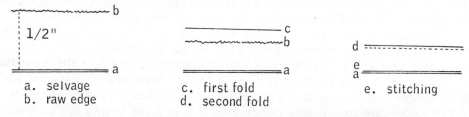

a. selvage
b. raw edge
c. first fold
d. second fold
e. stitching

FIGURE 9 - PREPARATION OF PULL FOR CASING

Run the completed pull into the casing.   This will be used to draw up the lower edge tightly for each fitting on the dress form as well as on the completed form.

Padding the Dress Form

1. General Directions

Place the muslin shell on the dress form and pin it carefully down the back observing the 1" seam allowance and the cross markings.   The objective for this fitting is to learn how the muslin shell made to the individual measurements, corresponds to the dress form, where padding must be added, and how to adjust the dress form.

The non-adjustable dress form is ready for padding.   The adjustable needs to have changes made to make it nearer the body measurements. While the shell is on dress form, check the length of the total waist length and the location of the bust line.   Adjust length from inside and fasten screws tightly.   Check girth measurements and extend the form the amount needed to leave the shell 3 1/2" to 4" larger than the dress form for foam padding and about 2" larger for cotton padding.   Fasten screws tightly.

Adjust the side seams of the shell so that they run straight and at right angles to the floor.   Observe:
a. length of dress form in relation to:
1. measurement (on Table 1) from shoulder to tip of breast or of shoulder blade
2. measurement from tip of breast or shoulder blade to waistline (Table 1)
b. areas where padding is needed
c. areas where little padding is needed
d. width of shoulder

2. Variations in Padding
a. With Cotton

If the shoulder pads are needed to raise the shoulder line because of waist length, fasten them firmly in place.   T-pins will hold them firmly.   If this does not make the shoulder firm enough replace the pads with strips of polyurethane foam graded on the under side to the proper shoulder slope. Foam pads, if used for large bust, will be placed later.

The use of the cotton for padding is the next step.   Begin with a wide, thin layer for all of the preliminary padding.   Cut one strip the size of the hip circumference by the length of the dress form from waistline to bottom. Place these on the dress form molding the cotton to the figure and the ends of the cotton strips together.   Pin them firmly to the dress form.   Repeat with several thicknesses of cotton in the areas located in 1-b and c on the preceding page.   Cover with the muslin shell, and pin it carefully down the back and draw it up snugly at the bottom.   Examine to see if there is excessive padding on any area, and to see where more padding is needed.   Take care to not have the padding too heavy at the neckline, at the waistline, and between the shoulders.

The shoulders need to be made firm and made the exact length of the individual's measurements. For this needed firmness or stiffening use manila folders, regular size. Use the front and back of the shell to cut a pattern for this stiffening. (See Figure 10.) Using the width of the shoulders given on the chart, Table 1, measure along the shoulder seam of the pattern pieces to the shoulder width minus 1" and mark this point. From this point draw a line curving down to the armhole seam both back and front. Cut two thicknesses of manila folder for each shoulder. Place these on the dress form and check the shoulder width again. Make any adjustment along the shoulders and armholes necessary to have them conform perfectly to the measurement of the shoulders and the shape of armhole of the individual. Pin the manila stiffening firmly in place. Use heavy office pins for all this work on the dress form, as ones used for dress-making bend easily. T-pins are good to fasten ends of manila stiffening into the papier-mache.

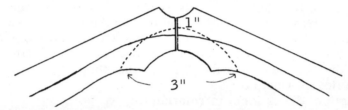

FIGURE 10 - MAKING PATTERN FOR SHOULDER STIFFENING

Some instructors use crushed tissue paper alone or combined with layers of cotton to pad a dress form. This is possible, but it will not result in as compact, stable a dress form as one padded with cotton alone.

Remove the shell, and continue with the padding in parts where needed. From this point on, the padding will be in smaller, possibly unrelated areas. No more cotton will be pinned to the dress form. It will mold to the other layers.

Use as large pieces as possible in order to avoid a bumpy surface. When it is ready for the next fitting with the muslin shell, cover the dress form with a thin, pliable plastic bag. This will prevent the cotton adhering to the fabric of the shell when it is removed to continue padding.

Pin the "falsies" into the muslin shell; pad the tips more, if needed, between the "falsies" and the muslin.

b. With Polyurathane Foam

This variation results in a firmer dress form and can be done in a little less time. It is not as easy as the cotton-padded one to stick pins into when draping is being done.

Check the measurement of the hips at the largest point. Buy this number of inches of 1" (thick) polyurathane foam. Measure from the waistline to 1 inch of the bottom of the dress form. Cut a strip of foam by these measurements less one inch in the circumference measurement. Tear strips of muslin 1 1/2 inches wide to use to fasten edges of foam together.

Pin the muslin on one lengthwise end of foam.

Place the piece of foam around the hips and pull around pinning the edges together at center back. At the side seams, cut out a wedge the length

of the hip curve. Pin edge together with muslin. Grade edges if needed.
Repeat the process by making smaller darts over the hip bones and at the
side back (below the shoulder blades). This should now fit the body contour.

Check the waistline measurement at top of the foam. If it is larger
than your measurement, grade the foam until it is the correct measurement.

Place the shell back on the dress form to check size through the rib
cage. If the foam was graded at the waistline in the hip area, it will need to
be graded in the lower part of the rib area. It may be that 1/2 inch thick
foam will be more suitable in the ribcage area for some dress form than the
thicker foam. The 1/2 inch could be used throughout and extra layers used.

Through the bust and shoulders, the thickness of the foam will be
determined by individual figure needs.

A thin layer of cotton will be placed over the foam.

Prepare manila pieces for the shoulders as on preceding page, Figure
10.

3. Suggestions for improving the padding:

Check the muslin shell on the dress form after each padding. When
preparing to stop work for the day, place the shell over the padding; pin
along back seam carefully; and tie at the bottom. This will help the padding
become more solid and compact.

Special attention should be given to particular areas during the padding,
for they are very likely to become over-padded or out of shape. These are:
(1) the midriff; (2) the waistline; (3) the underarm seamline of the blouse;
(4) the thickness of the back directly below the neck.

As the padding progresses, check the thickness and width of the form
with the squares and compare with your measurements at bust, hip and
waistline. (See Figure 5.) The dress form may measure correctly in girth
but be too thick or too wide. If this is true, the figure has become more
round than you are. Padding needs to be shifted to the side front in line with
the hip bones and in side back in line with the shoulder blades. The cotton-
padded dress form may be rolled with the hip area on a table (not the bust
area) to make it flatter; the foam padded will have to be graded to make it
smaller.

During the padding the manila folders on the shoulders may tend to
curve down. To correct this cut another strip of foam 2 1/2" wide and 6"
long. Place this under the edge of manila thicknesses and pin to dress form
with T-pins at armhole. Now continue with padding.

Completing the Dress Form

When the padding is as firm as possible and the dress form corresponds
to your measurements, complete the armholes and neck as follows:
1. a. Complete the armholes by measuring the length and width. Cut two
        muslin pieces so that the above measurements, plus 2", are on the
        bias. Using one piece for each armhole, slide it under the edge of
        the armhole. Your shears held flat will be helpful for this. Clip the
        seam allowance of the armhole to the staystitching and fold under on

this stitching line. (Avoid curving the shoulder seam downward.)
Whip the folded edge down very firmly and neatly after the muslin
shell has been pulled taut over the chest and width of back.

   b.   Bring a blouse or dress which has a comfortable set-in sleeve (not a
shirt sleeve). Place it on the dress form with the armholes of the
two garments lying together at the sides and shoulder. Mark on the
dress form the depth of the armhole. (The shell was fitted snugly
underarm.)

2.   Complete the neckline by cutting a bias strip of muslin 3 1/2" wide and
6" longer than the neck measurement. Fold to half width and press
firmly. Beginning at center back, place the folded edge 1" to 1 1/2"
above the neck edge and pin it in place. Slide the lower edge of the bias
strip under the muslin shell, and carry it on around the neck on each side
to the center front where the ends will cross. Where the bias curves
around the neck, the lower edge over the shoulder curves will need to be
clipped to make it lie flat. Clip the neck edge of shell to the staystitching
and fold under along the stitching line. Sew the folded neckline edge
firmly to the bias strip, and sew along the top of the bias fold, fastening
it to the jersey covering the dress form.

Let the dress cotton-filled form stand unfinished for a number of weeks
while you are using it to learn the basic techniques of draping. This interval
will give the cotton opportunity to become more firm before the dress form
is completed. This interval, when you are learning basic designing and
fitting your products on yourself, will give you an opportunity to check the
accuracy of your dress form as well as the quality of your draping.

After the draping problems are completed, check the measurements of
the dress form again. Make any needed changes and then firmly sew the back
seam. Often the students find the circumference seams are slightly large.
Do not take the muslin shell off to correct this. Darts can be pinned in —
usually along a seam line — and sewed down firmly.

Mark the armholes and the side seams with embroidery thread in the
same manner used to show the circumference lines (hip, bust, and waistline) on page 14.

The qualities of a good dress form are: (1) accuracy, (2) firmness,
(3) neatness, and (4) quality of handwork. (See Appendix C.)

BIBLIOGRAPHY

Erwin, Mable and Kinchen, Lila, *Clothing for Moderns* (New York: The
     Macmillan Company, 1960).
Evans, Mary, *Draping and Dress Design* (Ann Arbor: Edwards Brothers,
     Inc. , 1941).
Hillhouse, Marion F. and Mansfield, Evelyn E. , *Dress Design* (Boston:
     Houghton-Mifflin, 1948).
Link, Nell Weymouth, *Precision Draping* (New York: Funk and Wagnalls,
     1948).

Unit Two
Basic Procedures of Draping in the Blouse Area

Designing by draping can be developed best by learning the basic procedures and then advancing to creative work. Basic procedures will be presented through the manipulation of the basic dart in the following pages of this unit. When these have been developed to use as tools, the student can progress to variations of the basic blouse and to original designing.

The first work in the blouse area should be done in tissue paper to develop an understanding of procedure before beginning draping on fabric. One blouse is enough to do in the paper and will require only a few minutes. Cut the tissue by the measurements in Table 2, and continue work according to the instructions in the following problems.

From draping in tissue the student advances to draping in muslin. A muslin with a yarn count of about 160 per square inch is preferred for this basic work. Five yards will probably be adequate for these practice problems.

In later work the student will want to develop a design in muslin of a hand similar to that of the fabric to be used in the proposed garment to produce a similar effect. After learning the basic techniques one should always do some preliminary draping with the fabric to be used in the finished garment in order to develop a "feel" for the fabric and an understanding of how it reacts to manipulation. After greater confidence is developed, the worker may prefer to develop the design directly in the fabric for the garment.

Each variation of the blouse front is made for one half the body only and is cut with a 1" seam allowance at center front unless the design dictates otherwise. In this way two halves can be basted to the back for fitting, thus avoiding the construction of the whole blouse for each problem. The one blouse back will be used for the fitting of the different versions of the basic blouse front. This fitting permits the worker to try the garments on herself so as to check on the accuracy of her dress form and her skill at draping before she progresses further.

If shoulder pads are in fashion and to be used with the garment, they must be pinned in place and the draping done over them. If the individual has one shoulder which requires building up to make it seem the same as the other, this padding must be done before the blouses are draped. From this padding she can tell the size and type of shoulder pad she must always make for this shoulder, if the right and left one are to give the same appearance.

TABLE 2 – MEASUREMENT CHART FOR PREPARING FABRIC LENGTHS
FOR DRAPING BASIC BLOUSES

Back
  Length
    on dress form
      length from top of thoracic vertebra
      to waistline . . . . $15\frac{3}{4}$

    add
      one inch for each seam
      one-half inch for ease in length
      two extra inches . . . . $3\frac{1}{2}$ inches

                                        Total $19\frac{1}{4}$

  Width
    on dress form center
      width from ~~side~~ seam to side
      seam on bustline level . . . . $18\frac{1}{2}$ $9\frac{1}{4}$

    add $5\frac{1}{8}$
      ~~one inch~~ for each seam
      two inches for normal ease . . . .   4 inches
                                        Total $22\frac{1}{2}$ $11\frac{1}{2}$

Front
  Length
    Measure from side of neck on shoulder
    to tip of breast and then to waistline . . . . $16\frac{3}{4}$

    Add $5\frac{1}{8}$
      ~~one inch~~ for each seam
      one-half inch for ease in length
      two extra inches . . . . $3\frac{1}{8}$ inches
                                                                           $19\frac{7}{8}$
  Width
    on dress form
      width from center front to side seam 10

    add $5\frac{1}{8}$
      ~~one inch~~ for side seam
   $5\frac{1}{8}$ ~~one inch~~ for center front seam
      two inches for normal ease . . . . $3\frac{1}{4}$ inches
                                        Total $13\frac{1}{4}$

Problem I: Basic Blouse Back

All draping should be done with the fabric right side out. This is no problem in muslin as it is reversible, but it is very important in fabrics having a right and a wrong side.

PREPARING THE FABRIC

Check Table 2 for measurements of muslin for the blouse back width and length. Tear the strip of muslin by these two measurements. Straighten the fabric so that the selvages and torn ends will lie parallel to the sides and ends of a table.

Guide lines are needed in the draping so as to insure the fabric's remaining grain true. This is done in the practice fabrics by pressing guide lines as follows:

1. Fold strip of muslin in half lengthwise. Press.
2. Fold in center crosswise, grain true. Press.
3. Unfold and make two additional vertical creases parallel to the center fold.
4. Repeat #3 in the filling direction.
5. Unfold and press lightly to remove stiff creases that could interfere with draping. This faint crease will still show grainline.

These must be absolutely true both warpwise and fillingwise.

Another method of marking grainline in muslin is by pencil lines. It is good but more time consuming and has no greater accuracy.

Either of these methods - marking grainline with creases or with lines - can be used *only* in practice fabrics. In the fabric for a finished garment, grainline must be marked by rows of bastings in threads of contrasting colors, unless there is a woven design or heavy yarn which marks the grainline.

TABLE 3 - MEASUREMENTS FOR NORMAL NECKLINE

I. From Table 1	
a. Circumference of neck.	$12\frac{1}{2}$
b. Width of neck	$4\frac{1}{4}$
c. Thickness of neck	$4\frac{1}{4}$
II. With Squares (Use as in Figure 5.)	
a. Depth of front neckline from upper end of shoulder seam to right angle opposite hollow of neck	$1\frac{3}{4}$
b. Depth of back neckline from upper end of shoulder seam to right angle opposite top of thoracic vertebra	1

Fill in I from Table 1. Use squares to find II.

NECKLINE CURVE

The next step is to cut out the neckline curve. Use measurements taken with the squares. (See Table 3.) Follow this procedure: (See Figure 6.)

1. Fold the fabric vertically in the center again and lay flat on table.
2. Allow 1" for shoulder seam.
3. Measure over from center fold one-half the neck width measurement and place dot on shoulder seam allowance. (See Table 3-Ia.)
4. Use the measurement on Table 3-IIb and mark on center fold plus 1" for shoulder seam allowance. Draw neckline by connecting these to points #3 and #4 and draw the back neck curve.
5. Add 5/8" seam allowance.
6. Cut neckline curve on this line.
7. Clip neckline curve.

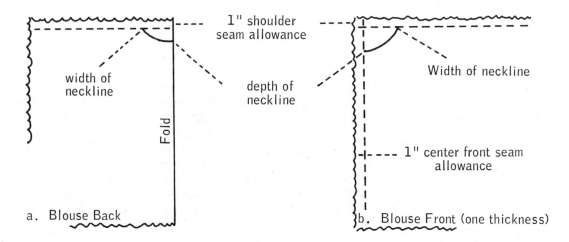

FIGURE 11 - CUTTING NECKLINE CURVE

DRAPING BLOUSE BACK

Place the unfolded strip of muslin on the back of the dress form allowing 1" seam allowance at the shoulders. Pin the center fold line of the muslin to the center back of the dress form by running the pins in straight. Do not stretch the fabric. Pin the neckline. It may be necessary to slit this slightly in the seam allowance to make the fabric lie flat. Smooth the fabric gently onto the form along the shoulders. The filling yarns must now be parallel to the floor at the width of the back line. Pin the shoulder seam to the French dart line.

At the midpoint of the shoulder make a small dart which will be about 1/4" to 1/2" wide. The exact size is determined by the curve of the shoulder, because the dart must straighten the grainline through the width of the back. The length also will be determined by the curve of the shoulders. Bring the dart to a point just above the fullest part of the curve. Smooth the material over the shoulders and pin the remainder of the shoulder seam.

On each side, just above the back bustline and slightly to the side of the shoulder blade, pin a vertical tuck, called an "ease-tuck", in the muslin 1/2" wide. Use only one pin for this and do not pin into the muslin shell. An ease-tuck will introduce the fullness needed in the completed blouse and will remain pinned until the blouse back is completely draped. (See Figure 12.)

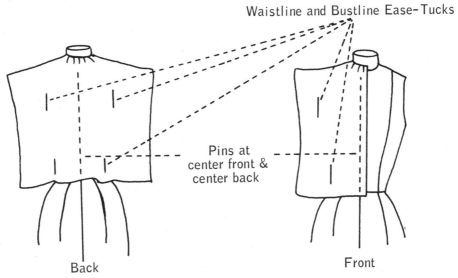

Waistline and Bustline Ease-Tucks

Pins at center front & center back

Back   Front

FIGURE 12 - EASE TUCKS

Complete marking the shoulder seam line from the French dart line to the armhole.

Mark the armseye by sticking pins straight into the padding at 1/2" intervals to mark the armhole lines.

A small amount of ease should always remain at the waistline to prevent any distortion of the grain in that area. To assure this, pin an ease tuck of 1/8" width at the waistline between the side seam and a point below the tip of the shoulder blades. This will remain pinned until the blouse back is completely draped. (See Figure 12.)

Pin vertical darts from the waistline toward the shoulder blades to take care of most of the excess material resulting from the difference in measurements of the back width at the bustline and at the waistline. Pin these two vertical darts equi-distant from the center back, directly under the location of the shoulder blades and pointing toward them. Place pins on each side of darts straight into the padding as was done on the neck darts. These darts should end 1" to 1 1/2" below the shoulder blades, depending upon the current fashion. At the side seam the warpwise yarns should be vertical or sloping very slightly toward the side seam.

The underarm seams will follow the matching seamline in the muslin shell. It will begin at the lower part of the armhole (marked with embroidery thread) and extend to the waistline in a ruler line. Place pins straight into the padding so the heads mark the line. Mark the waistline by running a row of pins straight in over the line of couching encircling the waistline. Now remove the pins holding the ease-tucks over the shoulder blades and at the waistline. The blouse back is now completely draped to conform with each side of the body and to allow for ease of movement.

MARKING SEAMS AND DARTS

Remove the muslin from the dress form by pulling it straight out from the form. The pins will remain as placed with heads on the right side of muslin. Place the muslin over tracing paper with the pin points down, and trace the darts and the seam lines on neck edge, armholes, and underarm. Use a ruler to draw all straight lines and a French curve to draw the curved lines. At the bottom of the blouse mark the waist line 1/2" lower than the row of pins to allow for minimum ease in length. Remove all pins. Add seam allowances of 1" at the shoulders, underarm, and lower edge and of 5/8" at the armholes and the neck. Cut out the blouse on these last lines.

Problem II: Basic Blouse Front

A. WITH UNDERARM DART

PREPARING THE FABRIC

Make this for the right side of the body, and plan to have it open down the center front. Check Table 2 for the length and width needed for the blouse front. Tear a strip of muslin by these two measurements. Straighten the fabric.

Turn under 1" for the center front seam. Press. Mark the grainline by pressing grain-true creases as done for the blouse back. Unfold and press lightly to remove the heavy creases which could interfere with draping. The slight creases that remain will still show the grainline.

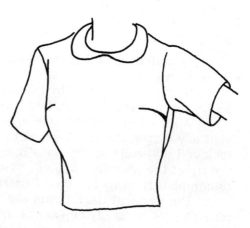

FIGURE 13 - UNDERARM DART

NECKLINE

Marking the neckline on the fabric is done as that for the blouse back but will be on one side only in the practice problem. (See Figure 11 b.) Use measurements taken with the squares. (See Table 3.)

Procedure:
1. Allow 1" for shoulder seam.

2. The center front seam has been turned under and pressed so measurements are from the center front.
3. Measure over from CF line half the width of the neck and place a dot on the shoulder seam line. (See Table 3-Ib.)
4. Use the measurement on Table 3-IIa. Mark this measurement on the center front line plus 1" for the shoulder seam. Draw the neckline by connecting points located in #3 and #4.
5. Allow 5/8" seam allowance and cut on this line.
6. Clip the neckline.

DRAPING

Place the fabric on the dress form leaving a 1" seam allowance at the shoulder and with the center front fold on the center front of the form, thus placing the lengthwise grain in position. Pin the center front, neckline, and shoulder seam lines. Be certain that the filling yarn runs parallel to the floor at the center front on the chest line and that the fabric lies smoothly but not stretched.

Slightly away from the tip of the breast toward the armhole but a little higher, pin an ease-tuck of 1/2" width as was done in the blouse back, Page 23. This is to allow ease and will remain pinned until the blouse front has been draped. (See Figure 12.) Mark the armseye.

Underarm darts begin at the underarm seam at a point 1/2" below the level of the tip of the breast and run up toward the tip of the breast ending 1" to 2" from the tip. (A slightly slanting dart is more flattering than one which runs straight.) This dart should make the filling yarns of the blouse below the dart run parallel to the floor. A person with a very large bust may have a smoother fit with two underarm darts rather than the usual one. The added dart makes it possible to have the folds shorter and thus fit the curve of the full bust better.

Place an ease-tuck at the waistline between the side seam and the point directly below the tip of the breast.

Run vertical darts from the waistline to a point 1" to 2" below the tip of the breast. These are equi-distant from the center front. This distance from the tip of the breast is determined by fashion. Make the vertical dart in the blouse wide enough to take up the difference between the bust and waistline measurements in this quarter of the blouse (except for the 1/8" ease-tuck).

Mark the underarm seam and the waistline with pins as was done for the blouse back. Unpin the ease-tucks. Remove the blouse front, and mark it with tracing paper as was done with the blouse back. Remember to lower the waistline seam 1/2". Add seam allowances as instructed for the blouse back.

B. WITH SHOULDER DART

Make this blouse half for the left side of the body so it can be used for fitting with the blouse made for the right side in A.

PREPARING THE FABRIC AND NECKLINE

Cut the fabric as in Problem II. Press under 1" at the center front and prepare the fabric as above in A. Mark and cut the neckline as in A.

DRAPING

Place the muslin on the dress form; pin at the center front, along the neckline, and along the shoulder seam to the French dartline. (The filling grain should be parallel to the floor.) At this midpoint of the shoulder, fold a dart which turns toward the neck and is large enough to straighten the grainline at the bustline level at the side seam as well as at the center front. The dart should terminate at a becoming point above the tip of the breast, but the exact length will be dependent upon the fullness of the chest and cannot be definitely located until the blouse is fitted.

Mark the remainder of the shoulder line.

Pin an ease-tuck 1/2" in width at the side of the bust and slightly above the bustline level. (The crosswise grainline will be parallel to the floor as the result of the shoulder dart.) Pin vertical darts, ease-tucks at waistline, armseye, underarm, and waistline seams as in A. Locate the armhole seam line and mark all with tracing paper as previously. Add seam allowances. Cut.

FITTING

Place staystitching on the two blouse fronts and on the blouse back as shown in Figure 14. Machine baste the darts. Pin the two fronts to the back; machine base the seams. Leave the blouse open in the center front. This is now ready for fitting to check the accuracy of the dress form and the draping. When the other blouse fronts are ready, the same procedure will be followed. (Have you observed directional stitching?)

Carefully determine if any alteration is needed in the blouse. If so, it may be due to the draping or to some inaccuracy in the dress form. Frequently adjustments are needed - squaring the ends of shoulder seams, removing a hump at the back of the neck, or adding cotton to make back shoulders curve properly.

C. WITH DIAGONAL DART AND CUT-ON FACING

In this problem the diagonal dart will replace both the underarm dart and the vertical dart. (See Figure 15.) It will have a cut-on facing to give the added experience.

A facing like this can be used with either of the blouse fronts described previously or on a blouse which opens in the back.

What: Stitching on all off-grain edges.
        The size of stitch varies with
        the fabric. Use that needed for
        plain stitching on the fabric.

Why: To keep off-grain edges from
        stretching.

Where: Place 1/8" from seam lines

Ease-stitch On Sleeve Top:
        Ease stitch is slightly
        longer than normal for the
        fabric. Begin at the top
        and stitch, to the notch,
        1/2" from the edge. At
        the notch decrease the
        size to normal and com-
        plete armhole stitching on
        the 1/2" line. On seam
        line (5/8") place a second
        row of stitching using the
        larger stitch and sew to the
        notches. Leave thread ends to
        pull up ease.

        Repeat the above on the second
        side of the sleeve.

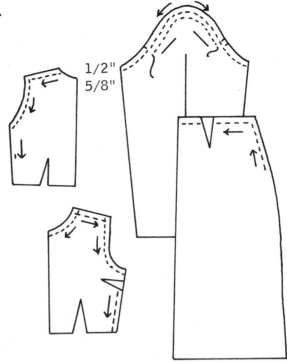

FIGURE 14 - STAY-STITCHING CHART - EASE FOR SLEEVE TOP

PREPARING THE FABRIC

Cut the muslin as for Problem II-A, but add 6" in width for the attached facing. (The 1" used in Problem II and III for the center front seam now becomes a 1" lap.)

Press a vertical fold in the muslin 7" from one side. This will be the center front. Unfold the fabric, then refold it so that the 6" allowance for the facing is turned under. This will remain this way during the draping. Note that the center front is 1" from the folded edge.

NECKLINE

Prepare the neckline as in Figure 11, but make all horizontal measurements from the center front line, not the fold line. The neckline will extend through the width of the center front lap.

DRAPING

Place the muslin on the dress form with the center front on the center of the dress form. This will allow for a 1" lap of the blouse front. Smooth gently in place and pin the neck, shoulder seam, ease-tuck, and armhole as in A.

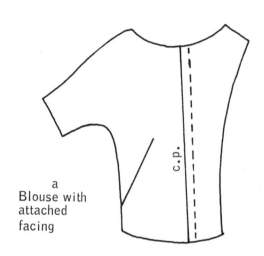

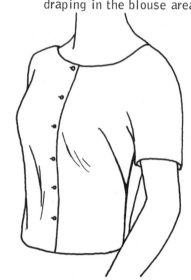

a
Blouse with
attached
facing

b

FIGURE 15 - BLOUSE WITH DIAGONAL UNDERARM DART AND CUT-ON FACING

A small ease-tuck will be needed at the waistline to allow the required ease. Place this tuck (1/4" in total) directly below the tip of the breast.

The diagonal dart will begin at the intersection of the waistline and underarm seams or slightly above the waistline seam and point to the tip of the breast, but will end 1" to 1 1/2" from the tip. It will replace both the conventional underarm dart and the vertical dart.

Two diagonal darts may be made rather than one, if desired. The second will begin at a point higher on the underarm seam and will end in the location given for the one diagonal dart. The lower dart will terminate below the tip of the breast and, usually, directly below the end of the top dart.

Fold the diagonal dart to control the material which would have formed the underarm and the vertical darts. It will turn down. Place pins on each side of the dart to mark its lines. Pin the underarm and the waistline seams. Unpin the ease-tucks. Pull the muslin from the dress form; mark the seam lines adding 1/2" length to the blouse as on the other blouses. Mark the seam allowance and cut out. (See pages 24 and 25 for seam widths.)

A diagonal dart will cause the filling yarns to run down at the underarm seam and warp yarns to run toward the side of the waistline. For this reason a diagonal dart should not be used on striped or checked material or one with pronounced filling yarns.

Fitting will be done as in Problem IIB.

After these practice problems have been developed and the fittings completed using the one back with two blouse front variations of the basic pattern per fitting, the student will be prepared to try her hand at variations in the basic blouse and at original designs. In these she will generally follow the same procedure. However, she may want to drape and pin baste simultaneously to develop the effect and the fit more quickly. For this the darts will not be pinned on each side for ease in marking but will be pinned flat. The side, shoulder, and armhole seams will be pinned to the dress form, trimmed, and then pinned together flat. The blouse can then have a pin fitting. Alterations may then be made; however, few alterations should be needed. By this time the dress form should be properly adjusted and the draping skill well developed.

The seam lines, darts, and center front will now be marked, and the pattern checked for accuracy of line.

Problem III: Set-In Sleeves

It is sometimes the practice to make an arm to use with the dress form. This is done by fitting a two-piece sleeve very snugly, stuffing it, and then closing the top and bottom. This is pinned onto the dress form at the shoulder. A sleeve can then be draped on this arm by observing grainline, height and width of cap, length, and underarm curve. The latter is the most difficult step.

As stated in the "Foreword," departure from draping techniques is advocated in a few places where experience has taught that the task can be accomplished more efficiently and accurately through the use of flat pattern. The sleeve is one example of this.

The most satisfactory method is to cut a plain sleeve by a commercial pattern of the size customarily used or to use the sleeve developed in a flat pattern course.

Cut the sleeves by the selected pattern. Place ease stitching as shown in Figure 14, and baste the darts and the sleeve seam.

Place the blouse on the dress form with the center front fastened, and pin the sleeve to the blouse with the underarm seams together. Pin at the top of the sleeve at the end of the shoulder seam with the vertical grainline hanging at a right angle to the floor. Ease in the fullness in the sleeve top. Pin the sleeve to the blouse with the filling grainline running parallel to the floor and with the sleeve hanging in straight lines on each side.

The sleeve should hang flat against the arm. If the center of the sleeve stands out as a shirt sleeve does, decrease the width of the top seam allowance until the sleeve hangs straight and flat.

If the sleeve has too much fullness across the top of the cap and at the side, the cap is both too high and too wide. Remove the sleeve from the blouse, and remove the ease lines. Replace these with new lines of stitching which leave wider seam allowances at the top and on the sides, but which will return to normal width when the stitching lines reach the underarm stay-stitching. Pin in place to the blouse, which is on the dress form. Repeat the draping for the second sleeve. Hand baste and fit.

Variations in the set-in sleeve will not be given, as they are done well by flat pattern method. (See the bibliography.)

BIBLIOGRAPHY

Erwin, Mabel, *Practical Dress Design*, (New York: The Macmillan Company, 1954).
Hillhouse and Mansfield, *Dress Design*, (Boston: Houghton-Mifflin, 1948).
Hollen, Norma, *Flat Pattern Method*, (Minneapolis: Burgess Publishing Company, 1961).

Unit Three
Basic Procedures for Draping in the Skirt Area

Each skirt is made for either the back or the front in learning the techniques of draping skirts. Two skirts, one front and one back, are basted together at the side seams with the upper left side open 7" to allow for fitting. This may result in fitting together two halves which are not harmonious in line. An example of this would be a straight skirt front with a flaring skirt back. Even though they are not harmonious, they can be fitted to check draping techniques and the accuracy of the dress form. Although the body shape differs greatly from front to back, the method of draping skirts for either is essentially the same.

TABLE 4

CHART OF FABRIC MEASUREMENTS FOR DRAPING SKIRTS	
Back	
Length (Desired length of finished skirt)	*17*
Add	
3" for hem	
5/8" for waistline seam	
2" for curve at waistline	5 5/8
Total	*22 5/8*
Width	
On dress form:	_____
Measure at 7" hipline the area to be draped.	
Add	
1/3 the above measurement	_____
1" for each side seam	_____
5/8" for gore seams	_____
2" for added fullness	_____
Total	_____
Grand Total	_____

Instructions for use:
   Fill in length of skirt from Table 1.
   All parts on width shown above will be figured in relation to the particular skirt being draped.

Problem I: Two-Gore Skirt
(Front only for practice problem)

PREPARING THE FABRIC

Use Table 4 to determine the dimensions needed in the muslin.

On this first skirt the procedure for finding the dimensions will be explained in detail and an example given (although all of this is shown in Table 4).

This problem is a two-gore skirt. The length is given on Table 1 and transferred to Table 4 and 5 5/8" are added. For example, if the finished skirt needs to be 20" in length, the total length will be 20" + 5 5/8" = 25 5/8".

The width of the lower edge of the skirt is determined largely by the fashion. For a slim skirt of moderate width add to the hip measurement, at the 7" line, one-third of the amount for the width at the lower edge. (For skirts above the knees one-fourth the hip measurement gives satisfactory fullness.)

The two-gore skirt has, of course, no center back nor center front seam; hence there will be two seam allowances of 1" for extra fullness on each side.

For a skirt front that measures 18" from side to side on the 7" hipline, the width needed is 18" + 6" + 2" + 2" = 28" for width of skirt panel (filling-wise).

Tear the muslin by these two measurements, 25 5/8" x 28". Straighten. Fold in the center lengthwise, grain true, and press. Mark the grainline by pressing as was done in the blouse problems. Unfold and press lightly to remove the stiffness of folds and yet mark the grainline.

DRAPING: (See Figure 16.)

1. Unfold the muslin and pin the center front on the dress form with 2" standing above the waistline.
2. Smooth the fabric gently toward the hips, keeping the filling parallel to the floor at the center area.
3. Fold two ease tucks, as was done in the blouse, on the 7" hip line two-thirds of the distance from the center front to the side seams. These need not be as large as in the blouse, if a slim skirt is planned. Take up 1/2" by making a 1/4" ease tuck. This will remain while the skirt is being draped.
4. Pin in an ease tuck of 1/4" total width at the waistline directly above the ease tuck at the hipline. (See #3 above.)
5. At the waistline directly below the tip of the breast form a dart which will take care of grainline and the difference between the waist and hip measurements. This dart will straighten the crosswise grainline, which should run parallel to the floor between the darts. (See Figure 12a.) Two darts should be used in place of one very large one, if the waistline is very small in comparison to the size of the hips. If a fuller skirt is

desired, the crosswise grainline will run diagonally downward toward
the side seam. (See Figure 12b.) The fuller the skirt, the more diagonal
the grainline becomes.

6. Smooth the fabric gently along the waistline and the sides. Pin the side
    seamline to the dress form down as far as the 7" hipline.

7. Without stretching the material, fold under 2" at the lower edge on the
    side seam, and let the seam slope up to the pins on the hipline. Check
    to see if this gives the desired effect. If a fuller effect is wanted, turn
    under only a 1" seam allowance on each side.

8. Remove the ease tucks at the hip and the waistline.

9. Repeat the above for the other side of the skirt.

10. Remove the muslin skirt from the dress form.

11. With tracing paper mark the darts, waistline, and hipline at the 7" line.

12. With a yardstick draw a ruler line from the point at the 7" hipline down
    to the lower edge of the skirt.

13. Mark the needed skirt length (see Table 4) plus 3" for hem allowance.

14. The hemline will curve up about 3/4" at the side seam. Draw the hem
    line.

15. Add the seam allowances (5/8" at waistline and 1" at side).

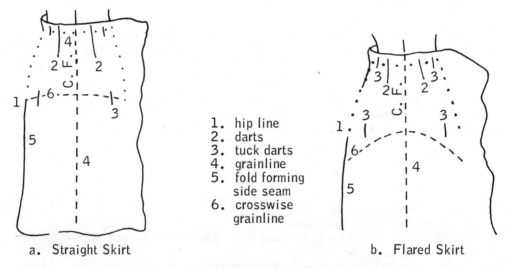

1. hip line
2. darts
3. tuck darts
4. grainline
5. fold forming
    side seam
6. crosswise
    grainline

a. Straight Skirt   b. Flared Skirt

FIGURE 16 - DRAPING A TWO-GORE SKIRT

A skirt back with no seams except at the sides rarely fails to take on
unbecoming lines after several wearings, as it takes on the line of the
derriere. For this reason the writer does not recommend a skirt back with
no seams, although it is often in fashion.

Stay-stitch the skirt as in Figure 14.

Baste-stitch the darts. When another skirt half is completed, machine
baste the side seams for fitting the skirt on the individual.

Problem II: Four-Gore Skirt
(Back only in practice muslin)

This skirt back will be used for fitting with the skirt front draped in Probelm I.

1. tuck darts
2. grain line
3. fold forming side seam
4. hip line
5. center back
6. waistline
7. hipline

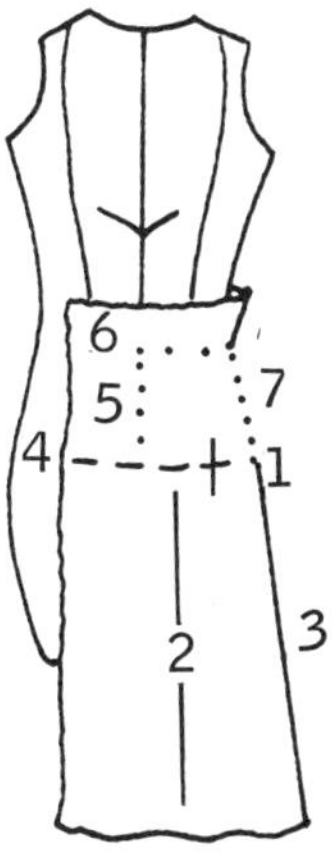

FIGURE 17 - DRAPING A FOUR-GORE SKIRT

Front
side
fullness
fabric needed fronts;
22 5/8
11

PREPARING THE FABRIC

Find the length and width as needed for one gore. (Note the differences in the amount added in comparison with Problem I.) For this skirt there will be 5/8" allowed for center back seam, 1" for side seam, and 1" for added fullness. (See Table 4.)

Tear two pieces of muslin by these measurements and straighten. Prepare the muslin as in Problem I.

DRAPING (See Figure 16.)

1. Unfold the muslin and place the fold line on the dress form away from the center front slightly more than half of the distance to the side seam. Pin on a vertical line, grain true, down 4". Drape each side of the skirt separately because of probable difference in hip shape.
2. Smooth the fabric toward the waistline, hips, and side. The crosswise grain will run down very slightly toward each seam. If the waistline is very small in relation to the hips, or if the person is swayback, a dart will be needed in each gore. Each will be located directly below the shoulder blade (or tip of the breast in a skirt front).
3. Pin the ease-tucks on the 7" hipline two-thirds of the distance from the center front to the side seam.
4. Pin the waistline, the side seams, and the center back seam down as far as the hipline.
5. Without stretching the material, fold under 2" at the lower edge on the side seam and let the seam slope up to the pins on the hipline. Check to see if this gives the desired effect. If a fuller effect is wanted, turn under only a 1" seam allowance on each side.

6. Measure at the hip line the distance from the center back to the fold in the center of the strip of muslin. To this measurement add 1/2". At the hem line of the skirt (not at the bottom) measure this amount from the center fold of the fabric toward center back; turn under the excess. This forms the center back seam. Because of optical illusion, a minimum of 1/2" slope of the seam is needed at the hem on a narrow skirt to avoid the appearance of this seam tucking in.
7. Remove the ease-tucks at the hip and waistline.
8. Repeat the above for the second side of the skirt. Place the notches on center back seam.
9. Remove the muslin skirt from the dress form.
10. With tracing paper mark the darts, waistline, and hipline at the 7" line.
11. Draw a ruler line for the center back seam from the waistline to the bottom of the skirt.
12. With a yardstick draw a ruler line at the 7" hipline down to the lower edge of the skirt.
13. Mark the needed skirt length (see Table 4) plus 3" for the hem allowance. Baste the two skirt backs together at the center with 5/8" seam width. Baste them to the skirt front with 1" seam width, but leave open 7" at the top of the left side.

Fit the skirt to check the accuracy of the skill in draping.

This skirt, with minimum flare, was draped to flow evenly down the center of the gore because the vertical grainline was pinned in a half way location between side seam and center. (See #1 above.)

If the effect desired is to have the flow or flare swing toward the side, the warp line will parallel the center front seam. If the skirt is full, the center front seam may run on a warp yarn. If the skirt is very narrow, it needs to have a slope of a minimum of 1/2" on the seamline at the center because of the optical illusion mentioned in #6 above. This will overcome the illusion of the skirt looking narrower than it does at the hipline center front.

If the flare is wanted at the front of the skirt, the warpwise grain line will parallel or nearly parallel the side seam. In medium full skirts which are fitted in the hip area, the side seams may run along the selvages up to the hip where they will curve to fit the curve of the hip.

Problem III: Six-Gore Skirt

(Back or front in practice muslin)

The width of the center front panel is a matter of choice or of fashion. It is well to keep in mind, however, that extreme difference in size between the center front and side panels tends to make the figure seem broader. The center panel made the width of that on the dress form will probably be the most becoming to the wearer. However, to learn the procedure in marking gore lines according to the individual design, a narrower panel will be made in this problem. With pins mark, on the dress form, vertical lines to indicate the width of the center front panel from the waistline to the 7" hipline. (See Figure 18a.)

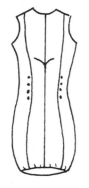

a. Marking width of
   the proposed center
   panel with pins

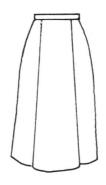

b. Completed
   front of a
   six-gore skirt

FIGURE 18 - DRAPING A SIX-GORE SKIRT

Find the length of the skirt on Table 4, page 30. Measure the width of the center panel at the hip line. To this add a minimum of 1" for optical illusion (1/2" on each side of the panel at the hemline) and 1 1/4" for seam allowances. Tear the muslin by the two measurements and prepare it for draping.

Measure the width of the dress form at the 7" hipline from the panel to the side seam. Using Table 4 find the dimensions of the side panels. Tear two pieces of the muslin by the measurements, and prepare them for draping the side panels.

DRAPING

1. Unfold the center front panel and pin the center front down to the hip line; leave 2" standing at top. The grainline will be at a right angle to the floor.
2. Smooth the fabric toward the side of the side panel with the crosswise grain parallel to the floor. Pin at the waistline and the sides of the panel down to the hip line.
3. Fold to the outside the 5/8" seam allowance at the bottom of the skirt. (This will allow for the 1/2" optical illusion; more than the minimum can be used for a fuller skirt. If the seam of a narrow panel is on the grainline at center front, the panel looks smaller at the lower edge. This statement is for added emphasis on optical illusion.)
4. Unfold the fabric for the side gore and place the middle, vertical fold two-thirds the distance from the center panel to the side seam and with 2" standing above the waistline. Pin the center of the panel down to the hip line.
5. Smooth the fabric gently along the waistline, hip, and the front panel line. Pin the tuck-darts at the hip line at about mid-point of the gore and at the waistline. If the individual has a very small waistline, in comparison to her hip measurement, a dart may be needed about in the middle of this panel.

6. Pin the waistline and the seam along the front panel as far down as the hip line.
7. Fold the lower edge of this seam to the outside 5/8" for the seam allowance and bring this fold to that of the center gore.
8. Fold under 2" at the lower edge of the side seam. Without stretching the material, let the seam slope up to the pins at the hipline. Check to see if this gives the desired effect. (Repeat 1-8 for the other side.)
9. Remove the ease-tucks at the waist and the hip line.
10. Remove the muslin skirt from the dress form.
11. Mark, with tracing paper, darts, waistline, and hipline to the 7" level.
12. With a yardstick draw the seam lines from the 7" hipline to the points established by fold in #8 and from waistline to points established in #3 and #7.
13. Mark the needed length (Table 4) plus 3" for the hem allowance.
14. Draw the hemline which will curve up about 1/2" to 3/4" on the side seam.
15. Add the seam allowances to each piece and cut.
16. Staystitch (see Figure 14) and baste the three gores together.
    This is now ready to baste onto another half skirt for fitting.

BIBLIOGRAPHY

Mary Evans, *Draping and Dress Design,* (Ann Arbor: Edwards Brothers, Inc. , 1941).

Marion S. Hillhouse and Evelyn A. Mansfield, *Dress Design,* (Boston: Houghton Mifflin, 1948).

Nelle Weymouth Link, *Precision Draping,* (New York: Funk and Wagnalls, 1948).

Unit Four
Variations in the Blouse Area

Some writers refer to the French dart line as the "princess line". In this writing the first term will be used, except for occasional references to princess line dresses.

All variations of blouse designs given in this unit will not be used for class problems. However, muslin will still be mentioned as the fabric. The worker may be using or adapting one of the variations for a garment rather than a practice problem in muslin.

Problem I:

A. BLOUSE WITH DESIGN ON THE FRENCH DART LINE

The French dart line is formed by joining the shoulder dart, which originates at the middle of the shoulder line, and the vertical dart in the lower part of the blouse. "The standard line is a slight curve entering (both) the shoulder and the waistline at right angles." (2) A more flattering, feminine effect can be obtained by beginning the dart farther out on the shoulder line, thus introducing a more curved line. (See Figures 20 and 23.)

In the blouse back the French dart line is formed by extending the shoulder dart to meet the vertical dart, thus giving a slight curve over the shoulder blades. This line also enters both the shoulder and waistline seams at right angles.

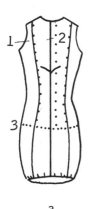

1. Pin heads marking design
2. Lap line
3. Lower edge of jacket
4. Width of front panel
5. Length of front panel
6. Width of side panel
7. Length of side panel

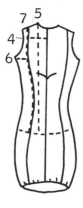

a   b

FIGURE 19 - DESIGN LINES AND MEASUREMENT GUIDES FOR JACKET

FIGURE 20 - FRENCH DART LINE DESIGN

FRONT

OUTLINING THE DESIGN ON THE DRESS FORM

1. On the dress form place a row of pins to mark the outline of the chosen design. Only the heads of the pins will show. (See Figure 19.)
2. Place a vertical row of pins on the left side 1" from the front. This will allow for a 1" lap for the blouse or jacket.
3. If this is to be a jacket, place a horizontal row of pins to mark the jacket length. (See Figure 20.)

PREPARING THE FABRIC

Make each side of the jacket in two parts, the front and the side front. (See Figure 21.) Block out the fabric for the front by cutting the length as outlined on the dress form; measure from the side of the neck to the lower edge of the jacket and add 1" for the shoulder seam and 1 1/2" for the hem. For the width of the front section measure from the point on the shoulder seam where the side front begins to the width of the lap. (See Figure 20b.) To this add 1 1/4" (5/8" for each seam allowance). Tear the muslin, straighten it, and mark the grainlines. Press under the 5/8" seam allowance on one long side. Fold this edge under a second time for the width of 1". Press and unfold. This last crease marks the center front. Allow 1" for the shoulder seam.

Cut the curve of the neck as in Figure 11, Page 22.

Measure the length of the side front from the beginning of the French dart line on the shoulder down to the bottom of the jacket. Add 2 1/2" (1" seam plus 1 1/2" hem). (See Figure 20b.) Measure the width of the dress form at the bustline level from the underarm seam to the French dart line. Add fullness as shown in Table 2 (3 5/8"). Tear the fabric and straighten. Mark the grain line.

DRAPING THE JACKET FRONT

1. Place the folded edge along the lap line with the remaining width extending over the opposite side of the body. Pin the center front line on the center front of the dress form leaving 5/8" seam allowance at the neck.
2. Smooth the fabric gently, straightening the crosswise grainline to a position parallel to the floor. Pin the neck and shoulder lines, the seam on the French dart line from the shoulder to the bottom, and along the lower edge of the jacket.
3. Place the side front on the dress form to allow for a 1" seam allowance at the shoulder.
4. Pin the middle of the side front to locate the grainline in the midriff area. The crosswise grain line will be parallel to the floor and the warpwise grain line will be at a right angle to the floor.
5. Pin the ease-tuck on the bustline.
6. Smooth the fabric gently and pin the shoulder and the armhole lines. (The grainlines will not be straight in this area.)
7. Ease the fabric slightly over the bust and pin the seam on the French dart line from the shoulder to the lower edge of the jacket.

8. Pin the side through the hip area allowing enough ease to take care of the design and the thickness of a skirt to be worn underneath the jacket. Mark the lower edge of the jacket.

9. The fullness at the midriff and waistline can be left as it is, or it can be darted out depending upon the effect desired and the current fashion.

10. Repeat steps 1-9 for the second side of the jacket front.

11. Unpin the ease-tucks.

12. Mark the matching notches at the seamlines on the French dart line.

13. Remove muslin from the dress form.

14. Mark the seams and darts and add the seam allowances.

15. Cut. (See Figure 21a.)

16. Baste and fit.

The four sections of the blouse front are now draped. (See Figure 21a.)

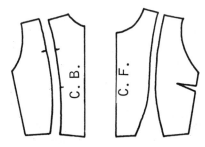
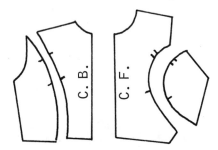

a. On true French Dart line   b. On variation of French line

FIGURE 21 - SKETCHES SHOWING SECTIONS OF BLOUSES DESIGNED
ON THE FRENCH DART LINE

BACK

OUTLINING THE DESIGN ON THE DRESS FORM

Follow the same procedure as for the blouse front. (See Figure 22b.)

PREPARING THE FABRIC

The jacket will be made in three sections: the center back and the two side back sections.

Block out the material by cutting the strip as outlined on the dress form. Measure from the side of the neck to the lower length of the jacket plus 2 1/2" (1" for seam allowance and 1 1/2" for hem). For the width measure the distance from one side of the center back panel to the other side. (See Figure 22b.) To this add 1 1/4" for the two seam allowances. Tear the muslin, straighten it, and mark the grainline.

Cut the back neckline as Figure 11, page 22.

Measure the length of the side back. (See Figure 22b.) Add the hem and seam allowances. (See Table 2 for additional width needed.) Tear two pieces, one for each side of the back. Straighten and mark the grainline.

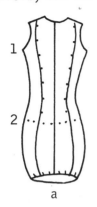

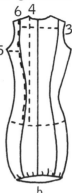

1. Pinheads marking design
2. Lower edge of jacket
3. Width of center panel
4. Length of center panel
5. Width of side back panel
6. Length of side back panel

a   b

FIGURE 22 - DESIGN LINES AND MEASUREMENT GUIDE FOR JACKET BACK

DRAPING THE JACKET BACK

1. Open the muslin cut for the center back of the jacket and place the center back fold on the center back of the dress form. Leave a 5/8" seam allowance at the neck.
2. Smooth the fabric, gently straightening the crosswise grainline of the panel making it parallel to the floor. Pin the neck, the shoulder lines, the seam along the French dart line from the shoulder to the bottom, and along the lower edge of the jacket.
3. Place the side back panel on the dress form to allow for a 1" seam width at the shoulder.
4. Pin the middle of the side back panel to locate the grainline in the midriff area. The crosswise grainline will parallel the floor, and the warpwise grainline will be at a right angle to the floor.
5. Pin the ease-tuck on the bustline.
6. Smooth the fabric gently, and pin the shoulder and the armhole lines.
7. Ease the fabric slightly over the shoulder blades (less than over the tip of the breast) and pin the seam on the French dart line from the shoulder to the bottom of the jacket.
8. Pin the side seams from the armhole through the hip area allowing enough ease to take care of the design and the thickness of a skirt to be worn underneath the jacket. Mark the bottom of the jacket.
9. The fullness at the midriff and at the waistline can be left in or darted out depending on the design and the current fashion.
10. Repeat steps #1-9 for the second side of the jacket back.
11. Unpin the ease-tucks.
12. Mark matching notches on the French dart line.
13. Remove the muslin from the dress form.
14. Mark seams, darts, and seam allowances.
15. Cut. (See Figure 21b.)
16. Baste to the jacket front.
17. Fit.

B. VARIATIONS OF THE FRENCH DART LINE

The number of variations possible is unlimited, both in the back and the front of the blouse. Modifications of the French dart line are used extensively in designs for suits, coats, and tailored frocks.

A more flattering, feminine effect can be obtained by beginning the dartline at a point farther out on the shoulder line or along the armhole. (See Figure 21b and Figure 23.) For example, the modified design may begin at the armhole, run to the tip of the breast, and then to the side seam, whereas in the back it may run from the armhole to the lower edge of the blouse. (See Figure 23e.)

If the French dart line passes between the armhole and the tip of the breast, the ease will be added to the center panel, often in the form of a dart. (See Figure 23b.) If the line passes over the tip of the breast, the fullness may be in the form of ease at the bust along the seam as in Figure 23a, c, and d or there may be a dart from the side seam as in Figure 23e.

Problem II: Variations through the use of Yokes

Yokes give endless opportunities for individual design. The shape of the simple yoke, the shape of the yoke in relation to the neckline, and the depth of the yoke in relation to the lower part of the blouse offer much freedom to the designer.

Fullness may be introduced into the lower part by pleats, gathers, shirring, and smocking. The shape of the yoke may be outlined by pin heads, or by another method — yarn or embroidery floss stretched and pinned to give the desired line. If the neckline is other than basic, mark it also with pins or yarn.

FRONT

PREPARING THE FABRIC

Measure the depth of the yoke from the highest point to the lowest and add 2". Measure the greatest width and add 2". Tear the fabric, straighten it, and mark the grainline.

Measure the length of the blouse from the point of the highest curve to the waistline. Add 4 1/2" to allow for seam allowances, ease, and possible curve. Measure the width from the center front to the side seam. Add the amount of fullness required by the design. Straighten the fabric and mark the grainline. Cut the curve of the neck. (See Figure 11, page 22.)

DRAPING THE FRONT

1. Place the fabric for the yoke on the dress form, smoothing it for true grainline; pin the neck, the shoulder, and the armseye (if in the yoke).

FIGURE 23 - VARIATIONS OF FRENCH DART DESIGN

FIGURE 24 - VARIATIONS IN BLOUSE AREA THROUGH USE OF YOKES

2. Pin the yoke on the design line. Block out the material along the pin lines giving somewhat the shape but leaving more than an adequate amount for the seam allowances.
3. Experiment with the fabric. If the lower blouse is to be gathered or shirred, determine the amount of fullness needed before tearing or cutting as suggested above. If it is to be pleated, try different sizes of pleats. When the width is selected, pleat the strip of fabric.
4. Place the section for the lower blouse on the dress form and pin it on the center front line.
5. Pin at the yoke line leaving the fabric as designed — straight, gathered, or pleated. No ease-tuck will be needed in the full blouses.
6. Pin the armhole, if it is part of the lower blouse.
7. Mark the waistline and the underarm seam. The underarm dart may have been thrown into the yoke line, thus making the omission of the underarm dart possible. The vertical dart may become pleats, tuck darts, or gathers.

BACK

PREPARING THE FABRIC

Take the measurements as instructed for the blouse front. Tear the fabric, straighten it, and mark the grainline.

DRAPING THE BACK

Drape the blouse back in the same manner that you draped the front.

Figure 24 shows a few variations in the blouse area through the use of yokes. In a the basic dart was thrown into the three radiating darts which came from under the yoke. It also has a gusset underarm in the kimono sleeve. (See Figure 31.) Notice that b has a very low neckline which results in the shoulder seam width forming caps over the shoulders. The center blouse front is a version of a long pointed yoke formed by a variation of the French dart line. Added interest is gained through the use of a contrasting colored fabric run through buttonholes.

Observe that c begins with a neckline lowered slightly. The yoke is rather narrow and of even width across the front and forms a band at the center front. The lower blouse front has two stitched tucks on each side of the center front opening. An ease-dart in the bust area would be needed for comfort in this design.

Sketch d, like sketch b, shows a low neckline. The yoke comes to the armhole line on the shoulders and widens as it approaches the dip in the center front. In e the center front of this low-neck, raglan sleeve blouse forms a yoke from which fullness radiates. (See raglan sleeve, page 60.)

FIGURE 25 - KIMONO SLEEVES

Problem III: Blouse with Kimono Sleeve

The kimono sleeve is cut in one piece with the blouse. It has more fullness through the shoulder and the upper arm area than a blouse with mounted or set-in sleeves. This fullness is to compensate for the lack of the armhole (which takes the place of this extra width in the set-in sleeve). (See Figure 25.) Without adequate fullness the kimono sleeve pulls out at the underarm seams; with too much it is baggy and often uncomfortable.

The width of fabrics available will permit making a short sleeve kimono blouse with a center fold in either or both front and back. However, a blouse with long sleeves will probably have center front and back seams, depending upon the width of the fabric. (See Figure 25.)

Draping of this type of sleeve requires a simulated shoulder-upper-arm area. To make a paper arm, cut a piece of heavy wrapping paper 36" by the measurement of the upper arm plus 3" (x inches). (See Figure 26a.) Roll up the paper lengthwise. (See Figure 26b.) The circumference at one end should equal the measurement of the armhole at the shoulder of the dress form. The circumference at the other end should equal the measurement of the bent elbow. Use plastic tape to hold the roll. Trim off the lower end to an even line, if necessary. (See Figure 26b.)

An arm can be made or muslin and stuffed with cotton; however, students usually work with greater accuracy in using the paper arm.

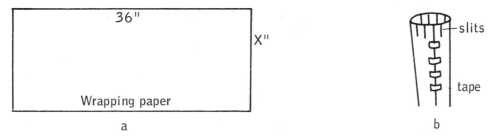

a   b

FIGURE 26 - PREPARATION OF THE SIMULATED ARM - SHOULDER AREA

Slit the larger end of this roll at 1/2" intervals, thus making tongues by which to pin the paper upper arm to the dress form. On each side of the taped seam, slit in from the edge 2" half the way around and slit in 1" the remainder of the roll. Pin the seam at the underarm with 2" slits on each side of it.

Fit this paper arm onto the curve of the armhole with the seam on the underarm seam of the dress form, placing the 2" slits along the lower part of the armhole and the 1" slits along the top. This will make the roll stand out from the mannikin at about the angle produced when one is standing with the hand on the hip. The sleeve will be about elbow length. (See Figure 27.) Pin the paper sleeve firmly in place.

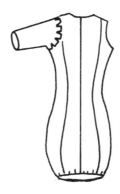

FIGURE 27 - PAPER SHOULDER-UPPER-ARM AREA

A. SHORT KIMONO SLEEVE

The directions below are for one-half a blouse back and front with short kimono sleeves. This half blouse, which is one of several to follow, will be fitted with another half blouse, as has been done with other practice problems. (See Unit Two.)

FRONT

PREPARING THE FABRIC

Measure from the center front at the neck, over the shoulder cap to the length desired for the sleeve. Mark this on top of the paper sleeve for use in working with both the back and front. Measure from the center front to the side seam at the bustline. Add to this 7" which will give 1" seam allowance at the center front and underarm, and the width and length needed for the short kimono sleeve. (Length - Table 2, page 20.)

1. Width from center front at neck to length of sleeve
2. Width from center front to underarm seam at bustline
3. Width of sleeve

FIGURE 28 - SHORT KIMONO SLEEVE

Measure the length of the blouse as instructed in Table 2, page 20. Tear the muslin, straighten it, and mark the grainline. Press under 1" for the center front seamline. If a normal neckline is desired, mark and cut it as shown in Unit Two. If another neckline is wanted, mark the design first on the dress form with pins or yarn, and then reproduce it by placing the strip of muslin on the dress form and by marking the new neckline.

To determine the width of the short sleeve at the lower edge, pin the tape measure in a circle. Slip the arm into this circle and hold it at the desired sleeve length. Check to see if this circle gives the desired sleeve fullness. When the amount is determined, find 47% of it. This will be the width of the sleeve front. (On a kimono sleeve the back area is the wider.)

DRAPING THE BLOUSE FRONT

1. Place the fabric on the dress form and pin the fold marking the center front. Smooth the fabric gently toward the shoulder and the armhole so that the grainline is straight through the chest area.
2. Pin the neckline and along the should seam to the French dartline.
3. Pin the ease-tuck at the level of the bustline but slightly forward of the tip of the breast.

4. Begin the underarm dart 2" lower on the underarm seam than the height of the bustline. Pin it so that it points to the tip of the breast, and straightens the crosswise grain.
5. Pin the vertical dart to take up the difference between the bust measure and the waist measure. Leave the usual 1/4" ease at waistline.
6. Pin the underarm seam from the waistline to the dart.
7. Mark the waistline.
8. Pin the shoulder seam to extend beyond the shoulder to the desired sleeve length. This line should not hug the shoulder cap but leave 1/4" to 1/2" ease in height.

     At this point leave the blouse front until steps 1 through 8 have been completed for the back.

BACK

PREPARING THE FABRIC

     To determine the crosswise measurement needed for the muslin, measure from the center back neck, over the cap of the shoulder to the length determined in front for the short sleeve. The blouse length will be found as instructed in Table 2. Prepare the fabric and the neckline as has been done for the blouse front above.

DRAPING THE BLOUSE BACK

1. Place the fabric on the dress form, and pin the fold at the center back. Smooth the fabric gently toward the sides; observe the grainline.
2. Pin the neckline and the shoulder seam to the French dartline.
3. Make the shoulder dart or an ease area on the shoulder the amount needed to straighten the grainline through the center and the upper shoulder area.
4. Make the ease-tuck in the shoulder blade area at the bustline level.
5. Make the vertical dart at the waistline. This will take in the difference between the bustline and the waistline measurements. Leave the usual 1/4" ease in each quarter of blouse at the waistline.
6. Pin the underarm seams along the side seams of the blouse front up to the underarm dart.
7. Pin the waistline seam.
8. Pin the shoulder seam to extend beyond the shoulder to the sleeve length marked on the arm. Leave 1/4" to 1/2" ease in height.
9. Complete the underarm curve by pinning the back and the front together, allowing the seam to curve 1" down from the location of a set-in sleeve. (Marked on the dress form page 17, 1b.)
10. Extend the seam for the previously determined length and width of the sleeve. In the completed sleeve the back should measure approximately 53% and the front 47% of the total of the lower edge.

11.   Remove the fabric from the dress form, mark the seam lines and darts.
      Add the seam allowances and cut.
12.   Baste to a second half blouse for fitting.
      If less deep curve is made at step 9 above, it may be necessary to use
a gusset.   A discussion of gussets follows in section D.

B. LOOSE THREE-QUARTER LENGTH KIMONO SLEEVE IN JACKET

Use the dress form with the paper shoulder-sleeve attached.

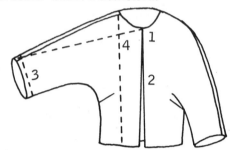

1.   Width from center front
     neck to length of sleeve
2.   Width from underarm seam
     to center front at bustline
3.   Width of sleeve
4.   Length of jacket.

FIGURE 29 - THREE-QUARTER KIMONO SLEEVE

FRONT

      Mark the length desired for the jacket in which the center fronts meet
but do not lap.

PREPARING THE FABRIC

      Measure on one's self the desired width from the center front, over the
shoulder cap to the length of the sleeve below the elbow, (see Figure 28) and
add 2".   Measure the length of the jacket from the shoulder to the bottom.
      Tear the fabric, straighten it, and mark the grainline.   Press under
5/8" along one side.
      Measure the width of the loose sleeve at the lower edge.   To deter-
mine the amount pin a circle with tape measure and, holding it at the desired
sleeve length, check to see if the width is pleasing.   (This jacket is designed
with normal neckline.)

DRAPING THE BLOUSE FRONT

1.   Place the fabric on the dress form and pin the fold marking the center
     front.   Smooth the fabric gently toward the shoulder and the armhole so
     that the grainline is straight through the chest area.
2.   Pin the neckline and along the shoulder seam to the French dartline.
3.   Pin the ease-tuck at the level of the bustline but slightly forward of the
     tip of the breast.
4.   Begin the underarm dart 2" lower on the underarm seam than the location
     of the bustline.   Pin the dart so that it points to the tip of the breast and
     straightens the crosswise grain.

5. Pin the vertical dart to take up the difference between the bust measure and the waist measure. Leave the usual 1/4" ease at waistline.
6. Pin the underarm seam from the waistline to the dart.
7. Pin along the lower edge of the jacket.
8. Pin the shoulder seam to extend beyond the shoulder curve to the desired length. This three-fourths length sleeve will be longer than the paper sleeve. Simply extend the sleeve seam in a ruler line to the length planned. The seams should not hug the shoulder cap but have 1/4" to 1/2" ease in height.

    A fitted facing will need to be cut for the jacket.

BACK

PREPARING THE FABRIC

Make the measurements for the back as you have for the blouse front. Prepare the fabric. Press under 5/8" for center back seam.

DRAPING THE BLOUSE BACK

1. Place the fabric on the dress form and pin the fold at center back. Smooth the fabric gently toward the sides; observe the grainline.
2. Pin the neckline and the shoulder seam as far as the French dartline.
3. Include in the shoulder dart, or the ease area, the amount needed on the shoulder seams to straighten the grainline through the center and upper shoulder area.
4. Make an ease-tuck in the shoulder blade area at the bustline level.
5. Pin the underarm seam along the side seams of the blouse front up to the underarm dart.
6. Mark with pin heads the lower edge of the jacket.
7. Pin the shoulder seam to extend beyond the shoulder to the sleeve length marked on the arm. Add 1/4" to 1/2" ease in height.
8. Complete the underarm curve by pinning the back and the front together, allowing the seam to curve down 1" from the location of a set-in sleeve. (Marked on the dress form page 17.)
9. Extend the seam for the previously determined length and width of the sleeve. In the completed sleeve the back should measure approximately 53% and the front 47% of the total of the lower edge.

C. LONG, FITTED KIMONO SLEEVES IN JACKET

Use the dress form with the paper sleeve attached. This jacket has a slightly lowered neckline and is similar to <u>c</u> Figure 54, page 93.

1. Length of jacket
2. Width of muslin
   for blouse front

FIGURE 30 - LONG KIMONO SLEEVE

FRONT

 Mark with pins the neckline, the lower edge of the jacket, and the width of the lap at front.

PREPARING THE FABRIC

 Measure on yourself the required sleeve length. This will be from the lap, over the cap of the shoulder, down the arm over the bent elbow to a point just below the knuckle on the little finger line at the wrist. Add 2 5/8" for facing seam and 2" for any change in plan.

 Tear the fabric, straighten it, and mark the grain.

 With the elbow bent take the circumference measurement and add 1 1/2" for ease. Determine length of blouse by Table 2, page 20.

DRAPING THE BLOUSE FRONT

1. Place the fabric on the dress form and pin the fold at the center front. Smooth the fabric gently toward the shoulder and the armhole so that the grainline is straight through the chest area.
2. Pin the neckline and along the shoulder seam to the French dartline.
3. Pin the ease-tuck at the level of the bustline but slightly forward of the tip of the breast.
4. Begin the underarm dart 2" lower on the underarm seam than the location of the bustline. Pin the dart so that it points to the tip of the breast and straightens the crosswise grain.
5. Pin the vertical dart to take up the difference between the bust measurement and the waist measurement. Now the lengthwise grain is straightened. Leave the usual 1/4" ease at the waistline.
6. Pin the underarm seam from the waistline to the dart.
7. Mark the waistline.
8. Pin the shoulder seam to extend beyond the shoulder curve and down half the length of the upper arm. This seam should not hug the shoulder cap but leave 1/4" to 1/2" ease in height.

BACK

PREPARING THE FABRIC

Make the sleeve length 1 1/2" longer than the front. Cut the blouse back length as shown in Figure 22.

DRAPING THE BACK

1. Place the fabric on the dress form and pin the fold at center back. Smooth the fabric gently toward the sides, observing the grainline.
2. Pin the neckline and the shoulder seam to the French dartline.
3. Make the shoulder dart, or an ease area the amount needed, on the shoulder seams to straighten the grainline through the center and the upper shoulder area.
4. Make the ease-tuck in the shoulder blade area at the bustline level.
5. Make the vertical dart at the waistline; this will take in the difference between the bustline and the waistline measurements. Leave the usual 1/4" ease in each quarter of the blouse.
6. Pin the underarm seam along the side seams of the blouse front up to the underarm dart.
7. Pin the waistline seam.
8. Pin the shoulder seam to extend beyond the shoulder curve and down half the length of the upper arm, leaving the usual 1/4" to 1/2" ease in height.
9. Complete the underarm curve by pinning the back and the front together, allowing the seam to curve down 1" from the location of a set-in sleeve. (Marked on the dress form page 17.)
10. On the sleeve back at the underarm seam, form one dart 1/2" in finished width about 5/8" above the elbow and another at the elbow. A third dart will be needed if the grain of the lower sleeve back will almost parallel that of the sleeve front. Place this third dart 5/8" below the dart at the elbow. The grain in this area should now run upward at the seam. This bias line is necessary for the sleeve to permit bending the elbow comfortably.
11. Complete the underarm and upper arm seams to a point just below the elbow darts. The approximate width of the back and front sections of the sleeve at this location will be as used before — the back 53% and the front 47% of the total. The elbow measurement was obtained on page 52 under "Preparing the Fabric. "
12. Complete pinning the elbow darts (see #9 above) so that they extend approximately two-thirds the width of the under panel (or back) of the sleeve.
13. Measure the top of the wrist from the side of the joint on the thumbline to the side of the joint on the little-finger line and add 1/4" to 3/8" ease. Measure the lower part of the wrist and add the same amount of ease. Extend the sleeve seam to the wrist where the top section of the sleeve will be just below and to the outer side of the joint on the little finger line.

14. Adjust the total sleeve width to the amount measured in 6. (Note that in the upper sleeve the back section is wider; as it approaches the wrist, the front section becomes wider.)
15. Remove the material, mark the seam lines and the darts. Add the seam allowances and cut.
16. Baste to a second half blouse for fitting.

D. GUSSETS

A gusset may be used to increase the underarm sleeve length, or it can be used to replace some of the fullness at the front and the back of the sleeve to give less bulk underarm. The different types of gussets accomplish different results.

There are several kinds of gussets that give satisfactory results. Two types with two variations of one follow. Gussets are discussed in texts for flat pattern.

TWO-PIECE DIAMOND-SHAPED GUSSETS

Use the kimono sleeve pattern. The advantage of the two-piece diamond-shaped gusset is that it gives the needed freedom of movement, but any excess ease can be removed by the curved seam underarm. (See Figure 24a and Figure 31.)

PREPARING THE GUSSET LOCATION

1. Use a kimono sleeve blouse pattern.
2. Place a dot on the shoulder seam one-half the measurement of the whole shoulder seam from the normal neckline.
3. Locate the middle of the underarm curve.
4. Place a ruler on the two points located in #2 and #3 and draw a line 3" long away from the underarm curve. Slash this line later. (See Figure 31a.)
5. Reinforce the area at the tip of the slash line. Use a very small stitch, 18-20 stitches per inch. Place several rows of stitching no farther than 1/4" from the side of the line. These rows of stitching will reinforce the area well and will not show when the gusset is sewed in place. (See Figure 31a.)

PREPARING THE GUSSET

Make a paper pattern as follows:
1. Fold a 6" square of paper to give a bias line.
2. Unfold and draw a line 2" from the edge and parallel to any side. This is the grainline for the gusset.

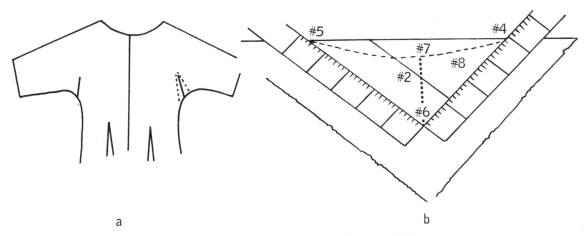

FIGURE 31 - TRIANGULAR GUSSET

3. Cut in two on the bias line and discard one piece.
4. Measure along the bias edge 1 1/2" and place a dot.
5. From this point established in #4, measure along the bias and place a dot 4 3/4" farther.
6. Using two rulers, adjust their positions so that one reads 3 1/4" from one dot, #4 above, on the bias line and the other reads 3 1/4" from dot in #5 above. Draw lines along these rulers from their point of intersection to the bias line. (See Figure 31b.)
7. Place a ruler from the intersection of these two lines, #6 above, to form right angles with the bias edge. Place a dot 3/8" from the bias edge. (See Figure 31b.)
8. Draw dotted lines from this dot, #7 above, to the points marked on the bias line in #4 and #5. (This removes some of the baggy effect.) Draw this grainline.
9. Add 5/8" seam allowances on all sides and cut four diamond-shaped gussets. Cut.

PLACING THE GUSSET IN THE BLOUSE

1. Slash the blouse from the armhole up to the top of the reinforcement at the slash line. (See Figure 31a.)
2. On the blouse back, place one straight edge of one gusset along the slash line, and bring it to a point just at the top of the reinforcement. There will be a 5/8" seam on the gusset, but on the blouse the seam width will vary from the mere width of the stitching at the top to 3/8" at the arm hole.
3. Place the other straight edge into the blouse along the side of the slash line as in #2 above. Baste.
4. Repeat the same with the blouse front.
5. Make the side seam, which will hold the back, front, and the two gussets together.
   This blouse is now ready to fit with another half blouse.

FIGURE 32 - KIMONO SLEEVE WITH PANEL GUSSET

PANEL GUSSETS

This type of gusset is used on the kimono sleeve designs. It reduces the amount of underarm fullness, allows freedom of movement, and gives a very pleasing, tailored effect. The panel may be a part of the sleeve and have the gusset running into the underarm seam (see Figure 23), or it may be a part of the blouse with the point of the gusset running into the sleeve. (See Figure 32c and Figure 33c.)

PANEL GUSSET IN THE SLEEVE

Begin with a kimono sleeve blouse draped in muslin.

PREPARING THE GUSSET LOCATION (See Figure 33.)

1. Measure over from the neckline one-fourth of the normal shoulder width and place a dot on the back should line. (See Figure 33a, 1.)
2. Place a dot in the middle of the underarm curve. (See Figure 33a, 2.)
3. Place a ruler on these two points and draw a slash line 3" long up from the armhole. (See Figure 33b, 3.) Close the elbow dart if the sleeve is fitted, as it will not be needed in this area.
4. Measure back 1" from the underarm seamline at the lower end of the sleeve. (See Figure 33b.)
5. Draw the line connecting the points located in #4 above and the upper end of the slash line drawn in #3. (See Figure 33c.)
6. Mark notches in the sleeve and wedge the areas. (See Figure 33c.)
7. Place together the underarm seams of the back and the front and mark the mid point of the underarm curve on the blouse front to match that on the back.
8. Repeat #1 through #5 above for the blouse front.
9. Cut these wedges off, both back and front. (See Figure 33d.)

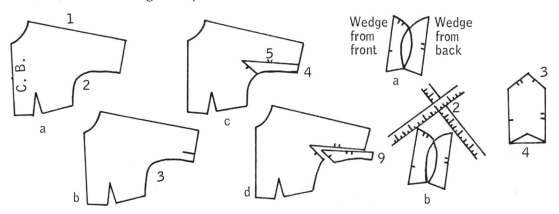

FIGURE 33 - PANEL GUSSET IN SLEEVE   FIGURE 34 - GUSSET

PREPARING THE GUSSET

1. Place the two wedges together at the lowest edge of the sleeve (1" apart on the short sleeve) and at the points underarm. Tape to paper. Draw a ruler line on the sides and the shape of the lower edge of the panel. (See Figure 34a.)
2. Following the method given in #6 on page 55, use two rulers (see Figure 34), but make each side of the point 3 1/4" (3" slash#line plus 1/4" reinforcement). Draw sides of the point. (See Figure 34b.)
3. Mark the notches. The notches down between the sides of the gusset point are moved to the lines drawn in #2 above. Note carefully that each notch is the same distance from the upper point of the gusset as it is from the armhole.
4. Shape the lower edge of the sleeve.
5. Add seam allowances on all edges.

PLACING THE GUSSET IN THE BLOUSE

1. Reinforce around the top of the slash line as for the diamond-shaped gusset in #5, page 54.
2. Close the underarm seam of the blouse.
3. Match the notches and baste the panel gusset in place. Note that the point of the gusset begins at the top of the underarm blouse seam and that the panel becomes part of the sleeve.
4. Close the sleeve seam.
   This blouse half is now ready to be attached to another blouse half for fitting.

PANEL GUSSET IN THE BLOUSE

PREPARING THE GUSSET LOCATION   (See Figure 35.)

1. Measure over from the neckline and place a dot on the back shoulder line at one-half the measurement of the normal shoulder width. (See Figure 35a.)
2. Place a dot in the underarm seam of the blouse.
3. Place a ruler on these two points and draw a slash line 3" long up from the armhole. (Steps 1-3 are a repetition of the process for Figure 33c, where the panel gusset is in the sleeve.)
4. Decide, by the design, how wide the side panel is to be and mark this width on the blouse. The width will be greater than that in the sleeve panel (See #4 in sleeve panel gusset above). There will be no underarm seam in this blouse. (See Figure 32c and Figure 35c.)
5. Draw a line connecting these two points (located in #3 and #4 above) and mark the notches. (See Figure 35c.)

6. Place together the underarm seams of the blouse front and back, and mark the mid-point on the blouse front to match the blouse back in #2 above.
7. Repeat for blouse front— #1 through #5 as outlined for back.
8. Cut these wedges off both the back and the front. (See Figure 35d.)

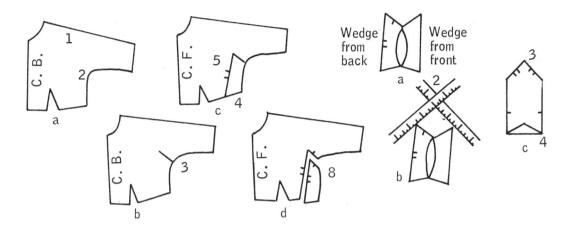

FIGURE 35 - PANEL GUSSET IN BLOUSE   FIGURE 36 - GUSSET

PREPARING THE GUSSET

1. Place the two wedges so that the side seams are touching. Tape the wedges on paper. (See Figure 36a.)
2. Following the method given in #6, page 55, use two rulers but make each side of the point 3 1/4" (3" slash line plus 1/4" reinforcement). Draw sides of the point. (See Figure 36b.)
3. Mark the notches. Move the inside notches to the outer edge of the gusset, measuring from the point. (See Figure 36c.)
4. Shape the lower edge. (See Figure 36c.)
5. Add the seam allowances.

PLACING THE GUSSET IN THE BLOUSE

1. Reinforce around the top of the slash as in the diamond-shaped gusset on page 54, #5.
2. Close the sleeve seams.
3. Baste the panel gusset into place. Note that the point of the gusset begins at the top of the slash line and that the panels become part of the blouse.
4. Close the panel-blouse seams.
   This blouse half is now ready to fit after being attached to another blouse half.

E. RAGLAN SLEEVE

The raglan sleeve has an underarm curve somewhat like that of a set-in sleeve, but it gives more fullness underarm. However, this fullness is less than that in a normal kimono sleeve. The shape of the upper part of the sleeve is completely different in shape from that of a set-on sleeve. (See Figure 37.) As seen in the sketches, the line runs from the underarm to the neckline and lends itself to many variations.

The design selected will be draped by the following instructions. (See Figure 37a.)

Mark the chosen design of the raglan sleeve, the neckline, and the blouse length on the dress form with pin heads or yarn. Decide on the width of the lower edge of the sleeve. As this sleeve is a variation of the kimono sleeve, use the paper arm.

PREPARING THE FABRIC

The length of fabric for both the lower back and the front is the measurement from the highest point of the design to the waistline plus 4 1/2". The width is from side seam to side seam at the bustline level plus 6". The material for the sleeve is cut on the bias the length from the neckline to the lower edge of the sleeve plus 3". The width is from the deepest part of the sleeve to the shoulder seam plus the seam allowances. Cut two for each sleeve.

Prepare the fabric for draping after it is torn; straighten and mark the grainline. The back will have a seamline and a slide fastener.

FRONT

DRAPING THE BLOUSE (See Figure 38a.)

1. Open the fabric and pin the blouse on the center front seam after the neck has been cut the shape designed. (See Figure 37a.)
2. Smooth the fabric gently to straighten the grainline in the chest area, and pin the neckline as far as the design extends.
3. Form ease-tucks on the bustline at points nearer the center front than the tips of the breasts.
4. Pin the design line from the neck to the underarm seam leaving 1/2" to 3/4" ease in the underarm seam. Pin this design on each side of the blouse.
5. Pin the underarm darts and the waistline leaving 1" ease at the waistline seam. This blouse has a blouson effect.
6. Pin the side seam up to the underarm dart, leaving 1" more width; that is, do not pin it flat to the seamline, but leave this extra 1".
7. Place the length of the muslin cut for the front sleeve over the paper arm so that the grainline is parallel to the center front above the chest line but bias for the remainder of the sleeve length. Repeat for the second sleeve.

FIGURE 37 - RAGLAN SLEEVES

8. Pin the neckline from the raglan line to the shoulder line on each side.
9. Pin the shoulder seam to extend beyond the shoulder length to the desired length. This seam should not hug the shoulder cap but leave 1/4" to 1/2" ease in height.
10. Pin to mark design lines from the neck to the underarm seams (which should be about 1" lower than for set-in sleeves).
    Leave the front at this point and complete the back.

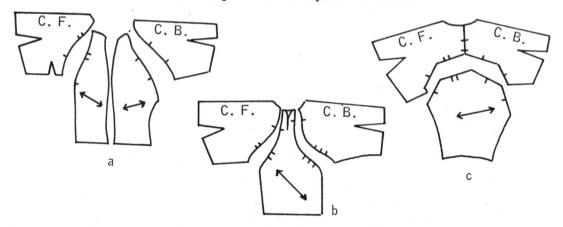

FIGURE 38 - SKETCHES OF RAGLAN, EPAULET, AND DOLMAN
SLEEVES WITH BLOUSE AREA

BACK

DRAPING THE BLOUSE

1. Pin the blouse back on the center back of the dress form after the neck has been cut the shape designed. (See Figure 37a.)
2. Smooth the fabric gently to straighten the grainline in the width of the back area. Pin the neck to the design line.
3. Form the ease-tuck on the bustline at a point nearer the center than the shoulder blades.
4. Pin the design from the neck to the underarm seam, adding a little ease (1/4" - 1/2" depending on the curve of the shoulder) through the shoulder blade area.
5. Pin the underarm dart. Leave 1" ease at the waistline for the blouson effect.
6. Pin the side seam up to the underarm dart on the blouse front and leave 1" extra width as in #6, page 61.
7. Place the length of the muslin cut for the back sleeve over the paper arm so that the grainline is parallel to center back in the width of the back area but is bias the remainder of the length.
8. Pin the neckline from the raglan line to the shoulder line.
9. Slope the seam over the shoulder cap leaving 1/4" to 1/2" ease in height as before. The seam will now run slightly forward.
10. Pin to mark the design lines from the neck to the underarm seams (which should be about 1" lower than for the set-in sleeves).

11. Complete the seam in the sleeve length making the width as planned above on page 60 with the usual 47%-53% relation between front and back. Complete the underarm seam to join the seam at the dart.
12. Remove the material from the dress form; mark the seam lines and the allowances. Cut.
13. Baste this blouse half for fitting with another blouse half.

There are many variations possible. For instance, in place of a seam down the length of the sleeve, the sleeve could be placed with warpwise grainline extending the full length and a dart used on the shoulder to fit out excess fabric. The dart will be similar to that on the shoulder of the epaulet sleeve, Figure 38b.

F. EPAULET OR SADDLE KIMONO SLEEVE

The procedure for this sleeve is quite similar to that for the raglan sleeve. As the name indicates, the upper or shoulder area forms an epaulet or saddle over the shoulder, and then the seams curve down in a manner similar to that of the raglan sleeve. (See Figure 38b and 39.)

With pin heads or yarn outline the design selected and then proceed as for the raglan sleeve. The fullness on the shoulders is usually placed in a dart or in the seams on either side of the epaulet. (See Figure 38b.)

G. DOLMAN SLEEVE

The dolman sleeve varies from the normal kimono sleeve in two particular ways: it has more fullness underarm, and it is cut separately. This separate sleeve, with its underarm fullness, gives much freedom for designing. (See Figure 38c and Figure 40.)

Mark the design selected on the dress form.

PREPARING THE FABRIC

Cut the length for the blouse as in Table 2. For width measure from the center front to the side seam at the bustline and add 6" or more, depending on how much underarm fullness is wanted.

For the sleeves cut two bias pieces of fabric the length needed to run from the top of the design to the length chosen. The width will be from the top of the sleeve design down, parallel to the front and opposite the lowest part of the design plus 3". Cut the muslin, straighten it, and mark the grainline. Cut neckline the desired shape and height.

Plan a center back opening for a zipper. Press under 5/8".

FIGURE 39 - EPAULET SLEEVE

FIGURE 40 - DOLMAN SLEEVES

FRONT

DRAPING THE BLOUSE FRONT

1. Pin the blouse at center front after you have cut the neckline according to the design.
2. Smooth the fabric gently to straighten the grainline through the chest. Pin the neck and the shoulder line along the design of the upper section of the sleeve.
3. Form an ease-tuck on the bustline at a point nearer center front than the tip of the breast.
4. Pin to mark the design line from the neck to the underarm seam leaving 1/2" to 3/4" ease in the underarm seam.
5. Pin the vertical and the underarm darts (if a dart is included in the design) and the waistline, leaving the usual ease for the latter.
   Leave the front at this point.

DRAPING THE BLOUSE BACK AND SLEEVES

1. Open the fabric and pin the blouse back on the center back seam after the neck has been cut the shape designed.
2. Smooth the fabric gently to straighten the grain in the shoulder area, and then pin the neck as far as the design extends.
3. Form ease-tucks on the bustline at points nearer the center back than the shoulder blades.
4. Pin the fabric around the neck and shoulder design of the sleeve.
5. Pin the vertical darts and the waistline, leaving the usual ease at the waistline.
6. Pin the side seam up to the dart on the front.
7. Pin together, lengthwise, the two bias pieces of the sleeve to form the shoulder-sleeve seam.
8. Place these two pieces (#7) with their seam meeting the shoulder seam of the center blouse front and center back. Bring down the arm to the desired length.
9. Pin the sleeve, following the marked design, to the underarm seam. (The blouse is eased at the bust and at the tip of shoulders, but the sleeves are not.)
10. At the underarm seam pin back and front together making the desired low curve.
11. Extend the seam to the end of the sleeve observing the 53%-47% proportion of the back and the front.
12. Remove from the dress form, and mark the seam lines and the seam allowances. Cut.
13. Baste and fit with another blouse half.

REFERENCES

1. Mabel Erwin, *Practical Dress Design,* (New York, 1954) p. 70.

2. Mabel Erwin and Lila A. Kinchen, *Clothing for Moderns* (New York, 1964)
    p. 357.
3. Norma Hollen, *Flat Pattern Methods*, (Minneapolis, 1961) p. 93.

BIBLIOGRAPHY

Bane, Allyne, *Creative Clothing Construction*, (New York: McGraw-Hill,
    1966).
Erwin, Mabel, *Practical Dress Design*, (New York: The Macmillan Com-
    pany, 1954).
Erwin, Mabel D. and Kinchen, Lila A. , *Clothing for Moderns*, (New York:
    The Macmillan Company, 1964).
Evans, Mary, *Draping and Dress Design*, (Ann Arbor: Edwards Brothers,
    Inc. , 1941).
Hillhouse, Marion S. , and Mansfield, Evelyn A. , *Dress Design*, (Boston:
    Houghton-Mifflin, 1948).
Hollen, Norma, *Flat Pattern Methods*, (Minneapolis: Burgess Publishing
    Company, 1961).
Link, Nelle W. , *Precision Draping*, (New York: Funk and Wagnalls, 1948).

Unit Five
Variation in Designing in the Skirt Area

The skirt designs which follow are all derived from the basic skirts presented in Unit Three. The variations may be an elaboration of one type of basic skirt, a combination of types, or an adaptation of one type to softer, fuller and usually dressier skirts.

Problem I: Pleated Gore Skirt

Pleats can be introduced at any gore line. The procedure which follows is based on a six-gore skirt, but the method will vary little for a different number of gores. The pleats may be parallel (the same depth from top to bottom) or they may be radiating (becoming larger at the bottom). The former gives a slenderizing, slimming line, while the latter gives a softer and usually a more graceful appearance. They may be pressed or unpressed.

A. SKIRTS WITH INVERTED PLEATS AT THE GORE LINE

This can be done with a skirt of any number of gores. The following instructions will be for the front of a six-gore skirt. The back will be made in the same way although the width of the panels will be different. The pleats may be pressed or unpressed.

METHOD ONE: INVERTED PLEATS BASED ON WAIST MEASUREMENT

By this method there is less bulk at the waistline, but the pleats do not lie flat in the hip area. It is better to use this method for unpressed pleats.

If the French dart line on the dress form gives the proportion wanted in the design, use these lines for the width of the gores and location of the pleats, then it will be unnecessary to mark the gore lines. However, if a different proportion is wanted for the season's fashions, mark the gore lines with pin heads. (Compare the proportions of the panels outlined in Figure 18a and b.)

PREPARING THE FABRIC

The instructions are for pleats on the center front panel plus one thickness of the pleat on the side gores.   This will place the seam line under a pleat rather than between the two pleats.   The advantage is that the seam is hidden.

Measure the front panel at the waistline.   Since all pleats have three thicknesses of fabric and since it was planned in the paragraph above to add one thickness of the pleat on the side gore, multilply by four and add 1 1/4" for the width of the two seam allowances.   The two pleats on the center front panel will turn away from each other (see Figure 41) and be one-half the width of this panel.   Do not let the pleats overlap.

Find the skirt length on Table 4.   Tear and straighten the muslin.   Fold in the center and press.   Complete the marking of the grainline as done previously.   (Remember that the grain will be marked by bastings if the fabric is not for a practice problem.)

The width for the side panel is the measurement at the waistline, from the center front panel to the side seam.   Add the pleat width at the waistline plus 1 5/8" for the seams.   Prepare two side panels by these dimensions (length and width).   Straighten and mark the grainline.

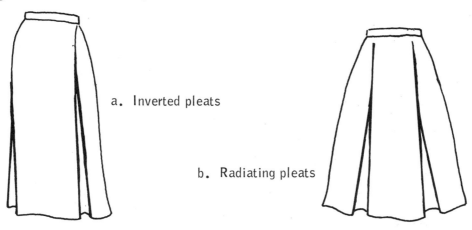

a. Inverted pleats

b. Radiating pleats

FIGURE 41 - PLEATED GORE SKIRTS

DRAPING THE SKIRT

1. Place the center of the front panel on the dress form and pin down the center to the hipline, but leave 2" standing at top.
2. Form the complete pleat of the desired width on each side of the panel. (Do not let pleats overlap.) The excess will extend to the sides.
3. Measure the same depth of the pleat at the hip and lower edge and pin the pleats.
4. Place the middle of the fabric for the side gore about half way between the center panel and the side seam.   Let it stand 2" above the wasitline.
5. Fold pleats at the hip and lower edge of skirt.   This will cover the excess of the center front panel.
6. Smooth the excess of the center front panel under the side panel, thus completing this pleat.   This will place the seam under the pleat.   Pin together the seam lines of the two gores.

7. Smooth the fabric gently along the waistline and the hip. Pin the waistline and hip. It may be a little snug in the hip area, but the pleats, when released, will take care of this.
8. Repeat #4-7 above for the other side gore.
9. Fold under 2" at the lower edge on each side seam and let the seam slope up to the pins on the hipline. Check to see if this gives the desired effect.
10. Mark the notches for matching seams, fold lines for the pleats, and pin the seam lines.
11. Remove the muslin from the dress form.
12. Mark with a yard stick and tracing paper the pleats, seam lines, and the seam allowances.
13. Mark the notches. If the pleats are to be unpressed, the pleat lines may be marked down only 4".
14. The hem will curve up 1/2" to 3/4" at sides.
15. Leave a 3" hem.
16. Cut, staystitch, and baste.
     This is now ready to fit with another skirt half.

METHOD TWO: INVERTED PLEATS BASED ON HIP MEASUREMENT

This method gives more thickness at the waistline, but the pleats at the hip area will lie flat. This is better than Method One if pleats are to be pressed. (Figure 41a.)

PREPARING THE FABRIC

Measure the width of the center front panel at the hips. Multiply by four and add 1 1/4" for seams as in Method One above. Find the length as in Table 4, page 30. Cut one.

The side panel is the width from the front panel to the side seam at the hip plus the width of pleat and seam allowances. The length is the same as for center front panel. Cut two.

Straighten the three panels, and mark the center and grainline.

DRAPING THE SKIRT

1. Place the center of the front panel on the center front of the dress form to the hipline, but leave 2" standing at the top.
2. Form the complete pleat the desired width at the hipline. (There will be in excess the width of the pleat and the seam allowances.) Fold the pleat to the outside.
3. Measure the same width of the pleat at the lower edge; form the pleats. (Excess as in #2, above.)
4. Place the fabric for the side gore with the middle about half the distance between the panel and the side seam. Let the fabric stand 2" above the waistline. Pin down the center of panel to the hipline.

5. Fold the pleat the same width as in #2, above. It should meet the pleat formed on the center panel at the hip and the hem lines. This will cover the excess on the center front panel.

6. Fold the pleats at the waistline, tapering from the width at the hip to the narrower width needed to fit the waistline at both the center and side panels.

7. Smooth the excess of the center panel under the side panel, thus completing this pleat. This will place the seam under the side pleat.

8. Pin together the two gores.

9. Smooth the fabric gently along the waist and hip lines.

10. Repeat #4-9 above for the other side gore.

11. Mark the notches on the seam lines, pleats, and seams at waistline and hip as far as the largest part.

12. Fold under 2" at the lower edge on each side seam, and let the seam slope up to the pins on the hipline. Check to see if this gives the desired effect.

13. Remove the muslin from the dress form.

14. Mark, with tracing paper, the pin markings in #11.

15. Mark the seam and pleat lines from the hipline to the bottom of the skirt using yardstick and tracing paper. Add the seam allowances.

16. The hem will curve up 1/2" to 3/4" at side.

This is now ready to baste for fitting with another skirt half.

B. SKIRTS WITH RADIATING PLEATS

Radiating pleats widen as they run toward the hem line. For example, a pleat may be 2" at the waistline but 3" at the hem. (Figure 41b.)

This type of pleat gives more fluid lines and a more graceful skirt. As with straight pleats, these may be pressed or unpressed.

Mark the gore lines of the design on the dress form or use the French dart lines. (See Figure 41b.)

PREPARING THE FABRIC

1. For the dimensions of the muslin for the center front panel, find the length, Table 4, page 30, plus hem allowance plus 4". For the width of the center front panel, find the measurement of the center panel at waistline. This will be divided into two pleats, one of which will turn to the right and one to the left. The pleat at the hem line will be at least 1" wider (1/2" for optical illusion on each pleat), but more will be needed for the pleats to radiate pleasingly. Multiply the total width of the two hemline pleats by four and add 1 1/4" for seam allowances. For example: if the panel at the waistline is to be 4" wide, it will result in two pleats 2" in width. The flare at the hem is to be 1" for each pleat or a total of 2" (4" + 2" = 6"). Hence the width of the panel is 6" x 4" + 1 1/4" = 25 1/4".

2. The width of the side gores is the hip measurement of the gores as marked on the dress form, plus one-third this measurement (for the slope of the side seam), plus 1 5/8" seam allowance, plus the width of the pleat

at the hem using, again, the example of the pleat width named above. If the side gore at the hipline measures 6", the width of the fabric for the side panels would be 6" + 2" + 1 5/8" + 3" = 12". The length will be the same as for the center front panel. Cut two.
3. Straighten the fabric and mark the grainline.

DRAPING THE SIDE FRONT PANEL (See Figure 42.)

1. Place the middle of the side gore half the distance from the center panel to the side seam allowing it to stand 2" above the waistline. Pin down the center to the hipline.
2. At the bottom of the edge nearer the center front, fold outward (with seam allowance to outside) the width of the pleat at the hem plus the seam allowance. Pin at the bottom only.
3. At the waistline smooth the fabric gently toward the center and fold outward at the gore line, forming part of the side pleat. Pin.
4. Fold the pleat from the waistline to the hem being careful that the fabric is not stretched (#2 and 3). Pin the fold of the pleat.
5. Repeat #1-4 for the second side panel.

DRAPING THE CENTER FRONT PANEL (Work on each side of center panel.) (Figure 42.)

1. Place the center front of the panel on the center front of the dress form and pin to the hipline, leaving 3" standing at the top.
2. Smooth the fabric toward the pleats of the side gores and toward the waistline.
3. Pin at the waistline.
4. From the point where the center gore meets the side gores measure twice the width of the pleat at the top.
5. Fold this point in #4 down to touch the side pleat. This forms a new pleat at the waistline, and the extension completes the pleat in the side skirt. Pin at the waistline.
6. At the bottom measure, from each outer edge, the seam allowance plus three times the pleat width. Fold and pin this to the pleat of the side gore.
7. Measure, from the fold in #6, twice the pleat width at the hem.
8. Fold, forming the pleat at the hem. Pin. The remaining amount completes the pleat on the side panel plus the seam allowance.
9. Fold the pleat from the waistline to the hem being careful that the fabric is not stretched (#5 and 6). Pin the fold of the pleat.
10. Smooth the fabric gently along the waistline and hip. Pin the waist and hip lines.

COMPLETING THE SKIRT

1. Fold under 1" at the lower edge on the side seams and let it slope up to the pins on the hipline. Pin at the bottom.

2. Repeat for the second side panel of the skirt.
3. Mark notches, pleats, and seams.
4. Remove the muslin.
5. Measure down from the waistline and add the hem allowance for all three panels.
6. Make the side seams and gore seams ruler lines below the hip area.
7. Mark all notches, pleats, seam lines, and seam allowances. Cut, stay-stitch, and baste.

    This is now ready to be fitted with another skirt half.

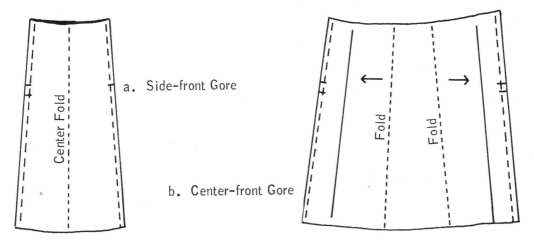

a. Side-front Gore

b. Center-front Gore

FIGURE 42 - RADIATING PLEATS IN SKIRT GORES

Problem II: Circularity in Skirts

Circularity is circular fullness or flare. Circularity in skirts causes the filling grainline to drop at the side lines of the gores, throwing fullness into the skirt and forming bias seams. Figure 16b shows the sloping grain-line of a slightly flared skirt. On a circular skirt this slope will be more extreme. The greater the circularity is, the greater the slope will be. (See Figure 43a.)

A. TWO-GORE CIRCULAR SKIRTS

Two-gore circular skirts are made, preferably, with the warpwise grain making the lengthwise line of the skirt. The width of the material, the fullness of the skirt, and the height of the wearer, but especially the first two, determine the direction of the skirt length. It is often necessary in a two-gore circular skirt to have the crosswise grain become the lengthwise line of the skirt; this is not preferable, as the warp line hangs better vertic-ally than the filling line. The alternative of the latter is to cut it warpwise and to piece the corners. (See Figure 43.)

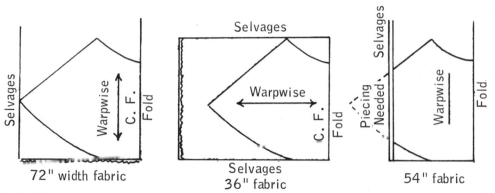

FIGURE 43 – PLACEMENT OF CIRCULAR SKIRTS IN RELATION TO FABRIC
        WIDTH

Figure 43 illustrates the problems encountered in planning a very full circular skirt. Each half of this two-gore skirt is approximately 2 1/2 yards at the bottom. The three drawings show how the fabric would have to be treated with a skirt of this fullness.

Determine the desired width for the lower edge of the skirt. (A study of counter pattern books will give this.) Divide by two, and mark this amount, plus 3", on the fabric with a pin. Do not cut until later.

MEASURING THE FABRIC

Find the length measurement needed for the skirt front plus 2" for a hem. (Table 4, page 30.) Measuring up from the bottom of the uncut fabric, place the point of this measurement at the center front waistline, and let the excess width or length of uncut fabric come up over the blouse. (Both length and width remain uncut until you have done this trial draping.)

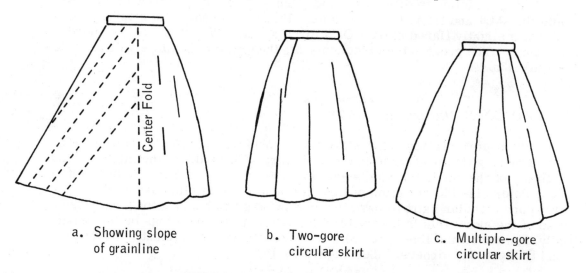

a. Showing slope   b. Two-gore   c. Multiple-gore
   of grainline   circular skirt   circular skirt

FIGURE 44 – CIRCULARITY IN SKIRTS

PREPARING THE FABRIC

1. Pin the fabric with the center front on the center front of the dress form at the measured length from the lower edge (length of skirt plus 2").
2. Mold the curve of the waistline, letting the fabric drop at the sides to form bias seams and the desired width of the skirt. Pin.
3. Examine to see if the desired circularity has been achieved. If not, add or substract to the slope of the grainline as may be needed for the desired effect. When the desired effect has been developed, check the width needed.
4. Cut the fabric by measurements found in #1 and #3.
5. Straighten and mark the grainline.

DRAPING THE FABRIC

1. Pin the fabric with the center at the center front of the dress form.
2. Mold to the curve of the waistline, cutting and slashing as needed to make the fabric lie flat and hang bias at the sides.
3. Mark the waistline leaving the usual ease-tuck.
4. Fold the side seam from the waistline to the hem taking care to not stretch the fabric.
5. Measure the skirt length on the side seams to match the center front.
6. Remove the fabric from the dress form.
7. Using tracing paper and wheel, mark the waistline, side seams (ruler line from top to bottom), seam allowances, and the curve of the hem, making it the same length from center front to side seam.
8. Cut.
9. Repeat for the back, or fit with another half skirt.
10. Staystitch and baste for fitting.

B. MANY-GORED CIRCULAR SKIRT

The procedure presented for the two-gore circular skirt can be used for any number of gores. Mark the number of gores wanted on the dress form. (See Figure 18 and 44c.) Divide the total width at the lower edge by the number of gores to find the width of each gore. Check the length on Table 4, page 30. In draping treat each gore as the front and back were treated in the two-gore skirt above.

If the skirt is to be close-fitting through the hip area and flare below, divide the number of gores into the total measurement at the hem line. (Find this measurement from a counter book of a commercial pattern company where a similar skirt is illustrated.) This will give the width needed at the hemline for each gore. Drape the skirt panels close, fit them down the desired distance, and introduce the flare at this point. (See Figure 42b.) Place the grain in the center of each gore and pin the center of the gore at right angles to the waistline to make the skirt flare evenly.

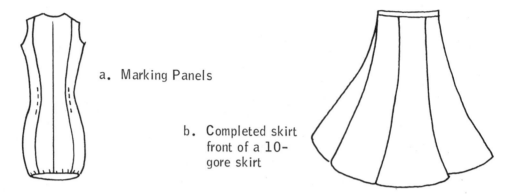

a. Marking Panels

b. Completed skirt
   front of a 10-
   gore skirt

FIGURE 45 - DRAPING A MANY-GORED SKIRT FITTED THROUGH THE
HIPLINE AND FLARED AT LOWER EDGE

Problem III: Free Designing in Skirts

As suggested in the introduction of this unit, much freedom exists in designing skirts. If one knows techniques for the basic skirts (Unit Three), plus the suggested variations found in this unit, much individuality of design is possible.

Figures 46, 47, and 48 show many ideas for variations. In the pages which follow, the individual sketches of skirts are discussed in relation to basic skirts or to the variation on which their design is based.

FIGURE 46

Sketch a is made by following the instructions in Unit Three for the two-gore skirt. The stitched dart is replaced by three tuck darts. This increased hip fullness will make the bottom of the skirt narrower than the top. The draped skirt will be similar to Figure 48a, page 79.

The skirt with the side front opening, b, is made like a one-gore front except that the right side extends only to the dart location on the left side. The two sides, right and left, are identical, thus resulting in the lapped front.

Sketches c, d, and f, all show four gores in the front or back skirt. In the skirt back c radiating pleats are formed over the gore lines. (See Figure 41b.) In f the center seam is on the warp grainline. Radiating pleats at both the French dart lines and hip seam, plus the hip dart, give the fluid lines of this skirt. In sketch d the four gores fit to the hipline with a little more ease than a straight skirt and then continue to flare to the hem. Sketch e is a very full skating skirt. It can be made with two side seams. However, for a small child the width of some materials would permit making this a complete circle. (See Figure 48.)

FIGURE 46 - SKIRT VARIATIONS

FIGURE 47

The first step for sketch a is to divide the dress form into the desired areas to check the proper proportions. Each of the two tiers of the skirt is made like a one-gore skirt front with an A-line silhouette. The scallops add interest.

The two gore back seam in sketch b has radiating pleats turned toward the center back. (See Figure 42 and Figure 44c.) The side seams probably are along the selvage up to the hipline where it curves to fit.

Figure 18, Figure 44c, and the discussion on page 54 give the method for sketch c.

An interesting variation of a circular skirt is seen in sketch d. The design line of the left side of the skirt begins with the dart-seam section of the blouse front and runs down to form one skirt gore. Note the radiating pleat at the left side front of skirt.

Sketch e is similar to sketch a, Figure 46. The tuck darts are placed at center front and radiate slightly toward the side seams. This draped skirt would be shaped on the sides much like the sketch in Figure 48a except for the direction of the radiating darts.

FIGURE 47 - SKIRT VARIATIONS

variation in the skirt area

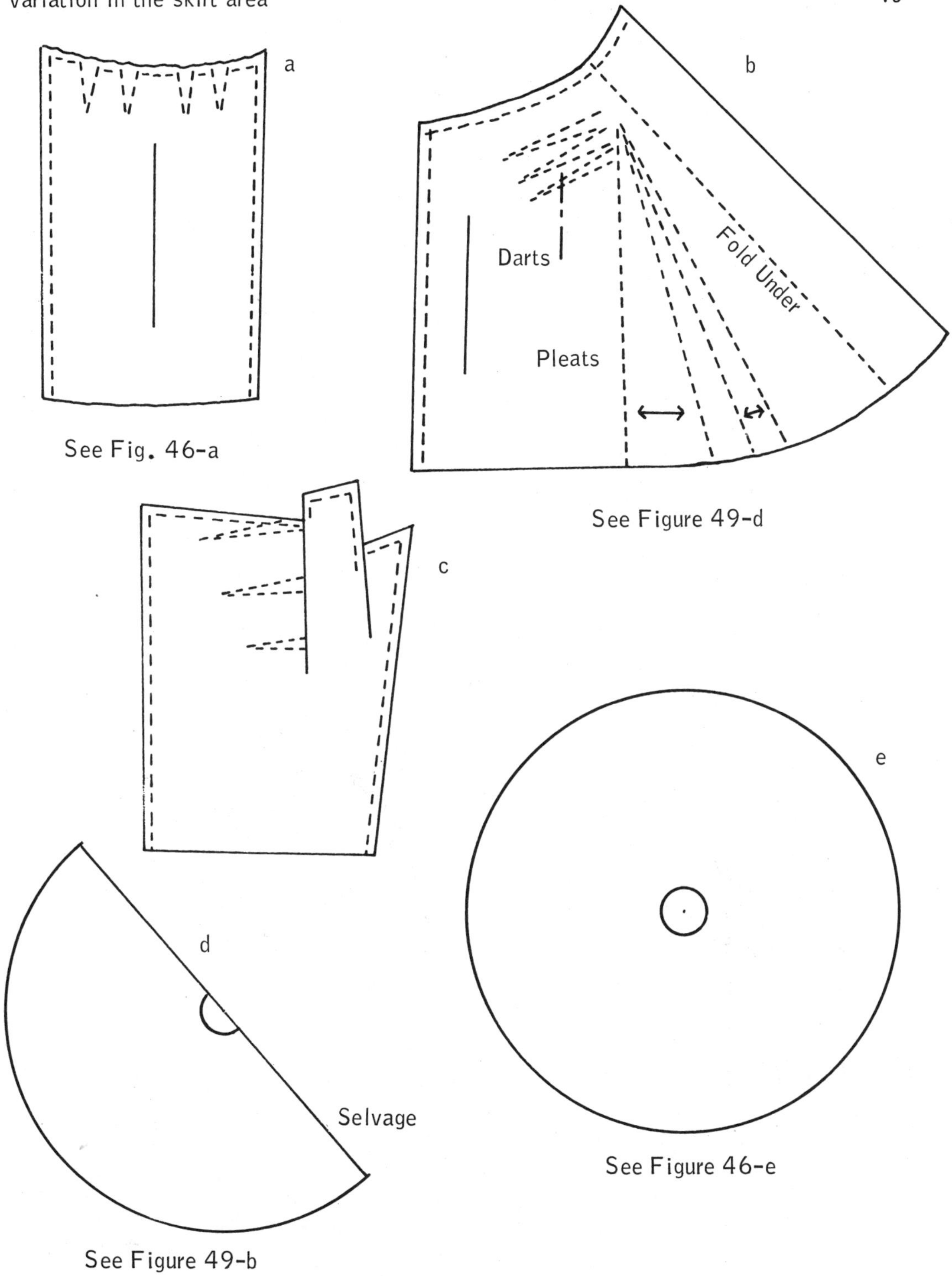
a
See Fig. 46-a
b
Darts
Pleats
Fold Under
See Figure 49-d
c
e
d
Selvage
See Figure 46-e
See Figure 49-b

(The designs, a, b, c, were draped to scale.)

FIGURE 48 - SKIRT VARIATIONS

FIGURE 49 - SKIRT VARIATIONS

The drawings in Figure 48 are drawn to a small scale. Drawing a is similar to the design that would result from the draping of Figure 46a and Figure 49c.

Drawing b is an interpretation of the design in Figure 49d. Drawing c illustrates how the sketch in Figure 49b could be draped.

The drawing in Figure 48d and e show two ways in which the sketch in Figure 46e can be developed. Drawing d would be used for narrow material which would not give the necessary length warpwise for a complete circle and would need side seams. Sketch e could be used in a wider fabric which would give the necessary skirt length.

FIGURE 49

Sketch a has a one-gore front with two large tuck darts on the left side-front. These form a point which rises above the lowered waistline. Sketch b has a similar treatment with tuck darts running into the blouse area. In addition there are diagonal skirt darts across the skirt front. Figure 48c was draped in a small size to give further help on this type of design.

Sketch c is a four-gore circular skirt with tuck darts controlling the fullness at the waistline. It would be shaped somewhat like e though probably more flared.

A pleasing draped effect can be achieved in a fabric which is soft and yet has body. (See sketch 49d.) There will be a complete one-gore skirt front which will show only at the far left side where the drapery ends. Drape the one-gore front on the right side. Each side seam will be straight or nearly so. The unpressed darts in the right side of the skirt will run across the skirt and end near the right side seam. The remainder of the right front forms long unpressed pleats and the graceful cascades. An ornament gives the finishing touch.

The wedding dress, sketch e, is very much like Figure 46a with tucks added at the waistline. In this dress the long skirt is shaped like Figure 48a but with greater difference in top and bottom width (the hip darts are larger and longer than on the other dress). The skirt back, which seems to form a short train, is draped like a circular skirt. This dress would need a complete skirt back with fullness like the skirt front under the train to hold the side seams straight.

BIBLIOGRAPHY

Erwin, Mabel, *Practical Dress Design* (New York: The Macmillan Company, 1954).

Evans, Mary, *Draping and Dress Design* (Ann Arbor: Edwards Brothers, Inc., 1941).

Hillhouse, Marion S. and Evelyn A. Mansfield, *Dress Design* (Boston: Houghton-Mifflin Company, 1948).

Hollen, Norma, *Flat Pattern Methods* (Minneapolis: Burgess Publishing Company, 1961).

Link, Nelle W., *Precision Draping* (New York: Funk and Wagnalls, 1948).

Unit Six
Collars

Collars are classified in several ways — according to style or silhouette, to degree of roll or lack of it, and according to the neckline shape.

In this unit the methods given will be, first, in relation to roll collars; second, instructions for shawl collars; third, adaptations of basic designs to give suggestions on creative designing.

The shape of the collar is very important to the success of the garment. It must be in harmony with the style of the garment; it must be in harmony with the size of the wearer; it must be becoming to the features of the wearer.

HEIGHT AND SHAPE OF THE NECKLINE OF A GARMENT

The method given for making the collar will have the neckline placed at the base of the neck. Some individuals do not like to wear a collar that comes up high in front and some may find it unbecoming. If one wants a collar that is dropped in front, or is further out from the neckline on the shoulder, or that has a lowered back, the change is very simple. Mark the desired shape and height with pin heads on the dress form, and proceed according to directions given for the normal neckline. Notice the different heights and shapes of necklines and of collars. (See Figure 50.)

THE SHAPE OF THE NECKLINE IN RELATION TO THE ROLL OF THE COLLAR

The shape of the neckline of the collar determines the amount of roll. The straighter the neckline of the collar, the higher it stands in back. As the neckline of the collar curves, the amount of roll decreases. The extreme of the first, the straight neckline, is the straight collar. (See Figure 50a.) (One that lies completely flat would be a fitted facing, not a collar.) The degree to which a collar hugs the neck is also affected by the shape of the neck. (See Figure 50b.)

DEFINITION OF TERMS

Several terms should be clarified before progressing further.

Stand refers to the distance above the neckline to which the collar rises.
Fall is the drop of the collar from the fold on the stand to the lower
edge of the collar.

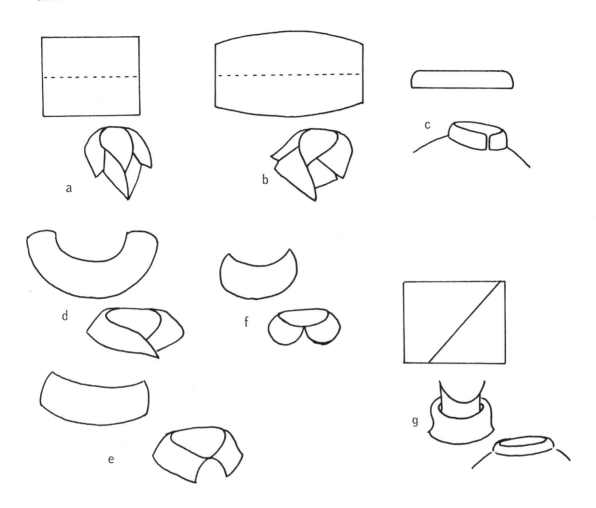

FIGURE 50 - SKETCHES SHOW SHAPE OF NECKLINES OF TYPICAL COLLARS

A *high roll* collar is one that comes far up on the neck in back. The
height chosen is influenced by the hairline and personal preference.

A *flat roll* collar is one that rolls very slightly, just enough to cover
the neck seamline.

An *intermediate* or *semi-roll* collar lies any place between the two
described above.

A collar which is the continuation of the lapel has a seam in center back.
This seam joins the two ends of the collar. It is called a *shawl
collar*.

Problem I: Flat Collar

The flat collar as defined above has very little roll, hence it has much
curve at the neckline.

PREPARING THE FABRIC

1. Measure the width planned for the collar at center back. Example: 2 1/2".
2. Pin the location at each side of the neck to which the collar should come on shoulders. Example: 2 1/2" from neck on each shoulder seam.
3. Place a tape measure across the shoulders directly below the thoracic vertebra, and measure the distance between the two pins. (Measurements were taken on the dress form of the writer.) Example: 9 3/4".
4. Find the thickness of the neck on Table 1, page 11. This is listed as depth of neck, a measurement taken with the squares. Example: 4 1/4".
5. Cut the material for the collar. Warpwise: two x collar width plus two x seam allowance plus the depth of the neckline. (See #4 above.) Example: 2 1/2" x 2" + 1 1/4" + 4 1/2" = 10 3/4".
    Fillingwise: Use the measurement found in 3 above plus 4" for ease and roll plus seam allowances. Example: 9 3/4" + 4" + 1 1/4" = 15".
6. Straighten the fabric and mark the grainline.

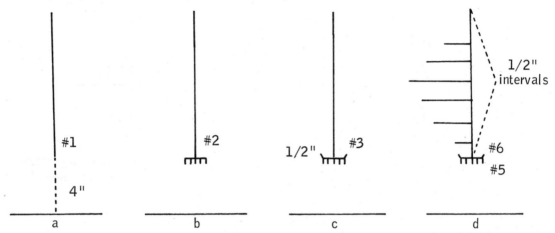

FIGURE 51 - PREPARATION FOR DRAPING A FLAT COLLAR

DRAPING A FLAT COLLAR

1. Cut the center warpwise fold from one end toward the other stopping back from the other end the desired collar width plus the stand plus the seams. The cut line will be referred to as "the slit." Example: 2 1/2" + 1/4" + 1 1/4". (See Figure 51a.) This allows 1/4" for height of stand.
2. Cut at right angles 1/2" from the fold at the end of the slit. Slash in 1/2" (toward the lower edge) along this line at 1/4" intervals. (See Figure 51b.)
3. Slash 1/2" diagonally at the end of the line cut above. (See Figure 51c.)
4. Open the fold and work on only one side of the collar. (See Figure 51d.)
5. Mark off at 1/2" intervals along the slit. (See Figure 51d.)

6. Slash lines at right angles to the slit as needed for the roll collar. For example: For a flat collar slash at right angles to the slit as follows:

> 1/2" from original 1" line - cut 1"
> 1" from original 1" line - cut 2"
> 2 1/2" from original 1" line - cut 2 1/4"
> 3" from original 1" line - cut 3"
> 3 1/2" from original 1" line - cut 2 1/4"
> 4" from original 1" line - cut 1 3/4"

7. Place the fabric on the dress form with the collar turned up on the neck and the seam allowance downward. Pin the neck and the seam allowance downward. Pin the neckline of the dress and the seamline of the collar together at the top of the thoracic vertebra for the width of the 1" slash.
8. Turn the collar down, with its stand above the seamline the amount planned. The example above was 1/4". (See Figure 50d.)
9. Pin the collar down to the dress form at the center back so that the stand remains during the draping of the collar.
10. Smooth the fabric toward the shoulder seam letting the filling yarns run upward on the shoulder about 1/2". The collar will now roll slightly, barely covering the neckline seam. Add more slashes if needed.
11. Bring the fabric around the neck so that it rolls gently toward the center front. Some of the slashes made in #6 above may need to be cut deeper to make the collar lie flat.
12. Stab pins to mark the neckline.
13. Shape the collar on the outer edge.
14. Remove the fabric from the dress form.
15. Fold in the center back, cut the second half of the collar adding the seam allowance.
16. Slash the neckline and fit the collar on the dress form. The collar should roll smoothly and lie flat on the shoulders.

Problem II: Intermediate Roll Collar

Intermediate or semi-roll collars have any desired amount of roll but have less than a straight collar and more than a flat-roll collar. This type, in its various forms, is probably the most popular. It is made very much like the flat roll, but the neckline will be straighter. (See Figure 50e.)

PREPARING THE FABRIC

1. Measure the width planned for the collar at the center back. Example: 2 1/2".
2. Pin the point on each side of the neck to which the collar should come on shoulders. Example: 2 1/2".
3. Place a tape measure across the shoulders directly below the thoracic vertebra and measure the distance between the two pins just above. (Measurements were taken on the dress form of the writer.) Example: 9 3/4".

4. Find the thickness of the neck on Table 1, page 11. This is listed as depth of neck, a measurement taken with the squares. Example: 4 1/2".
5. Cut the material for the collar. Warpwise: measure two x collar width plus two x seam allowance plus the depth of the neckline. (See #4 above.) Example: 5" + 1 1/4" + 4 1/2" = 10 3/4". Fillingwise: use the measurement found in #3 above plus 6" for the ease and the roll plus seam allowances. Example: 9 3/4" + 6" + 1 1/4" = 17".
6. Straighten the fabric and mark the grainline.

DRAPING THE FABRIC

1. Cut on the center warpwise fold from one end toward the other stopping back from the end the desired width plus a stand plus the seams. (See Figure 51a.) Example: 2 1/2" + 1" + 1 1/4" = 4 3/4".
2. Cut over 1" from the fold at the end of the slit. (See Figure 51b.)
3. Slash in 1/2" at 1/4" intervals along the 1" cut. (See Figure 51c.)
4. Slash upward 1 1/4" at about a 30° angle at the end of the 1" cut.
5. Open the fold and work on only one side of the collar. (See Figure 51d.)
6. Mark off 1/2" intervals along the vertical slash which extends to other end of collar.
7. Slash, as in Figure 51d, but use the figures below. However, omit the first 1/2" at right angles to the slit. Slash as follows:

> 1" from the horizontal cut - 2 1/4"
> 1 1/2" from the horizontal cut - 3"
> 2" from the horizontal cut - 3 1/2"
> 2 1/2" from the horizontal cut - 3 1/4"

8. Place the fabric on the dress form with the collar turned up on the neck and the seam allowance down. Pin the neckline of the dress form and the seamline of the collar together at the top of the thoracic vertebra for the width of the 1" slash.
9. Turn the collar down with its stand above the seamline the amount planned. The example being used is for 1".
10. Pin the collar down to the dress form at center back so that the stand remains during the draping of the collar.
11. Smooth the fabric toward the shoulder seams letting the filling yarns run upward toward the shoulder about 1/2". The collar will now roll.
12. Bring the fabric around the neck so that it rolls gently toward center front. Some of the slashes made in 6 above may need to be cut deeper to make the collar lie flat on the outer edge. Add more slashes if needed.
13. Stab pins to mark the neckline.
14. Shape the collar on the outer edge.
15. Remove the muslin from the dress form.
16. Fold in the center back, cut the second half of the collar adding seam allowances.
17. Slash the neckline and fit the collar on the dress form. The collar should roll smoothly and lie flat on the shoulders.

Problem III: Full Roll Collars

A. STRAIGHT COLLAR

This is also called a standing collar.

PREPARING THE FABRIC

1. Measure with a tape measure around the neckline at the base of the neck for finding the length needed for the collar.
2. Determine the amount of rise and fall desired and multiply by two. Add the seam allowances. (The lower edge of the fall can be a seamline.)
3. Tear the muslin by measurements found in #1 and #2.
4. Straighten the fabric and mark the grainline.

DRAPING THE FABRIC

1. Clip the neck edge. Fold lengthwise if the fall of the collar is on a fold. (See Figure 50a.)
2. Place the fabric around the neck pinning the seam line to that of the neck. Begin at center back and work each way.
   This collar stands very close to the neck in back. See Figure 50a with the drawing of the shape of collar and neckline. It may be worn open or closed at the neck.

B. CONVERTIBLE COLLAR

This type of collar is very popular in sports and semi-tailored wear.
The height may be as great as the straight collar, A, but it hugs the neck more closely at the sides. (Figure 50b.)

PREPARING THE FABRIC

1. Measure the width planned for the collar at center back. Example: 2 1/2".
2. Multiply the width by two and add two seam allowances.
3. Find the circumference of neck on Table 1, page 11.
4. Add two seam allowances to the collar length.
5. Fold the collar lengthwise and place a dot 1/2" up from the lower seamline at each end of the collar.
6. Take the measurement, on the dress form, of the back neckline from shoulder to shoulder. Mark this off on the center back of the collar.
7. Draw a line connecting the dots marked in #5 and #6. This forms a concave curve at the neckline.

DRAPING THE FABRIC

1. Fold the collar and clip the neck edge of both thicknesses of the collar.
2. Place the collar around the neck of the dress form beginning at the center back and pin it to the shoulder seam. Work on one half of the collar only.
3. Bring the collar to the center front and pin the neckline to hold it in place.
4. Turn the collar up to the standing position, and mark the seamline with pencil dots. Note that the collar is less wide in front than in back.
5. Remove the collar.
6. Fold at the center back and cut the sides and ends of the two thicknesses to match.
7. Add seam allowances at the neckline and the ends of the collar.
8. Slash the neckline, place the collar on the dress form, and fit. (See Figure 50b.) This collar may be worn open or closed.

C. MANDARIN COLLAR

A mandarin collar is one that stands high and has no roll. It may meet in center front, as the Oriental usually wears it, or it may have a space between the two ends at the lap of the blouse. (See Figure 50c.) The collar will be lined to stand stiffly, if the Oriental effect is desired.

PREPARING THE FABRIC

1. Measure the neckline.
2. Determine the height of the stand. Add two seam allowances to the width (height) of the collar. Cut two. (The collar may be cut with a fold at the top, but Oriental collars are made with a seam and stiff interfacing.)
3. Straighten and mark the grainline.
4. Place a dot 1/2" above the neckline at the end of the collar.
5. Take the measurement, on the dress form, of the back neckline from shoulder to shoulder. Mark this off on the center back of the collar.
6. Draw a line connecting the dots marked in #4 and #5. This forms a concave curve at the neckline.

DRAPING THE FABRIC

1. Slash the neckline in center back and over the shoulders.
2. Place the collar around the neck beginning at center back and pin as far as the shoulder seam. Work on one half the collar only.
3. Bring the collar to the center front and pin the neckline.
4. Shape the end of the collar.
5. Remove the collar.
6. Fold at the center back and cut the two sides of the collar to match.
7. Add the seam allowances.

8. Slash the neckline, place the collar on the dress form, and fit it. (See Figure 50c.)
   This collar will fit closely at the sides and back.

D. *TURTLE NECK COLLAR*

A turtle-neck collar is one made of a bias folded strip to give both stand and fall. Raise the front neckline 1/4" to 1/2" for a better line. A typical turtle-neck folds down the amount of the stand and is a full-roll collar which fastens in the back. (See Figure 50g.)

The collar may be a full circle joined, on the grainline, if the neckline has been lowered enough to make it unnecessary to have a back opening.

Problem IV: The Divided Collar

A divided collar is made in much the same manner as other roll collars, except that it rolls at the side neck and extends from front to back. One is made for each side. The height of the roll wanted will determine whether the method of a flat collar or a semi-flat collar is followed. (See Figure 50f.)

PREPARING THE FABRIC

1. Measure the width (crosswise grainline) planned for the collar at the side of the neck on the shoulder plus the amount of roll plus seam allowance plus 2" for ease and roll. Example: 2 1/2" + 1/2" + 1 1/4" + 2 = 6 1/4".
2. Check Table 1, page 11, for the measurement of the depth (measurement taken with squares). The warpwise length will be this depth plus the length of the collar at the center back and the length at the center front plus seams. Example: 4 1/2" + 2 1/2" + 2 1/2" + 1 1/4" = 10 3/4".
3. Cut the fabric, straighten it, and mark the grainline. You will need four collars.

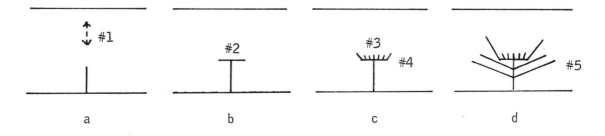

FIGURE 52 - PREPARATION FOR DRAPING DIVIDED COLLAR

DRAPING THE FABRIC

1. On the crosswise fold cut from one side toward the other stopping back
   the desired collar width plus the stand width plus the seam allowances.
   Example: 2 1/2" + 1/2" + 1 1/4" = 4 1/4". (See Figure 52.)
2. With the fabric still folded, cut 1/2" across at a right angle to the end of
   slit. (See Figure 52b.)
3. Cut back from this 1/2" at 1/4" intervals toward the edge of the collar.
   (See Figure 52c.)
4. Cut 3/4" diagonally at the end of the horizontal slit. Have this slash toward the collar area. (See Figure 52c.)
5. Open the fabric. Working on the half of the collar designated as the back,
   at 1/4" intervals cut slashes 2" and 2 1/2" respectively to parallel the
   diagonal line cut in #4 above. Begin the first slash down 1" from the
   horizontal line. (See Figure 52d.)
6. Repeat #5 above for the front half but have the slashes 2 1/2" and 3"
   respectively.
7. Place the fabric on the dress form with the center fold at shoulder line
   and with the collar lying on the neck, seam downward. Pin here at the
   shoulder.
8. Turn the collar down so that it stands above the seamline the amount
   planned. Example: 1/2". (See Figure 50f.)
9. Pin the collar down on the neck so the stand remains during draping.
10. Smooth the fabric around the neck both back and front so that it rolls
    smoothly. The grainline will become somewhat diagonal. If the slashes
    are not long enough, extend them.
11. Stab pins in to mark the neckline.
12. Shape the collar by marking or pinning.
13. Remove it from the dress form.
14. Add the seam allowances.
15. Clip the neckline and fit.
16. Two collars will be needed, and each will have two thicknesses. (Cut 4.)
    They will need interfacing also.

Problem V: A Shawl Collar

This collar is called a "collar band attached to the lapel" by some
writers. A blouse front is made with the collar attached. (See Figure 53,
55c and e, and the definition on page 83.)

PREPARING THE FABRIC

1. Measure the length of the blouse front from the side neck to the waistline.
   Example: 17".
2. Add 4 1/2" (as in Table 2, page 20) plus the width of the back neck from
   the shoulder seam to the center back plus the seam allowances.
3. Find the width of blouse half in Table 2, page 20.

4. Add to 3 above the width of the lap at the center front plus 2" for the shaping of the collar. Example: 14" + 2" + 2" = 18".
5. Cut, straighten the fabric, and mark the grainline.

DRAPING THE FABRIC

1. Measure back from the lengthwise edge the width of the lap plus 2" for shaping; fold and press the fabric. This marks the center front. Unfold the fabric. Example: 4".
2. Place the center front on the center of the dress form leaving 1 1/2" below the waistline and the remainder over the shoulder.
3. Bring to the shoulder seamline and pin maintaining the correct grainline through the chest area both in the warp and the filling directions.
4. Pin the shoulder seam, ease-tuck, underarm and vertical darts, and the underarm, armhole, and waistline seams.
5. Measure from the shoulder seam at the neckline to the center back at the neckline.

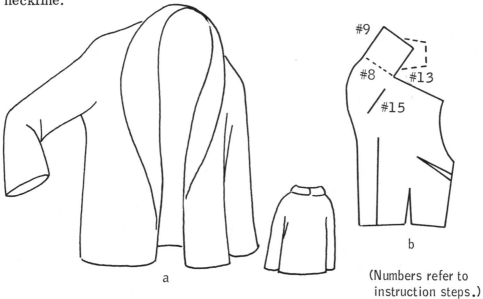

a

b

(Numbers refer to instruction steps.)

FIGURE 53 - SHAWL COLLAR

6. Remove the muslin and mark all the seams, darts, notches, and the center front.
7. Lay the collar flat on the table and lay the ruler in a position to extend the shoulder seamline, in its present slope, the amount measured in #5 above. Mark a dot.
8. Raise the location of this dot 1/2" and draw a dotted line from here to the end of the shoulder seam. It should measure the amount found in #5 above. (See Figure 53b.)
9. At the point established in 8 draw upward at right angles a line equal to #5. (See Figure 53 #9.)

10. Using this same measurement, #5, complete the square, thus returning the shoulder line. (See Figure 53b.)
11. Add the seam allowances to the shoulder and the square collar formed in back (except on dotted line).
12. Cut out the collar square and shoulder seam.
13. Clip the corner through the seam allowances where the shoulder seam meets the square. (See Figure 53 #13.)
14. Pin the shoulder seam and the collar (the square) around the neck and pin at the center back.
15. Form a diagonal tuck under the collar to take out excess fullness. (See Figure 53b #15.)
16. Turn the collar down over the diagonal tuck and experiment with the shape of the outer edge of the collar and the lapel. Mark the seam lines.
17. Remove the fabric, mark the darts, notches, and all remaining seam allowances.
18. Cut and baste.
    This blouse is now ready to fit with another blouse half.

Problem VI: Variations Based on Basic Collar Designs

Figures 54 and 55 show a number of collar variations. These are all based on collars discussed in the first part of this unit.

FIGURE 54

The collar a is derived from the turtle neck collar, although it may be difficult to recognize. In making this, the neckline back and front would be outlined with pins. At the center front the line would need to be raised slightly. Determine the needed length and width and drape. (This collar may have a seam on the edge.)
Collar b is a partial roll cut low on the back neckline, very wide at the sides, and low in front.
Collar c is also a turtle neck, but it laps and ends at the left shoulder.
Collar d is somewhat like collar b but shaped differently at the front neckline.
Collar e could be made by a straight piece of fabric folded on edge, by a bias folded in the same way, or it could be a flat roll collar with pleats introduced at intervals. Probably the second method, with the bias, would be the most pleasing, but the other methods should be tried, without cutting the fabric, to see which is most effective.

FIGURE 55 .

Collar a is another version of a turtle neck collar. It overlaps to one side and the right side is lowered.

Collar b is an intermediate or semi-roll collar similar to b on Figure 54. On each of these the lowered neckline, both back and front, would need to be designed first.

Collars c and d are both collars attached to the lapel. In d part of the lapel is removed to form the band. Sketch e shows how the collars are seamed in center back.

Collar f is very attractive. The collar back is cut on the bias, shaped at the shoulder seams, and stiffly interlined to make it stand properly. The collar front may be a part of the coat front.

FIGURE 54 - COLLARS

FIGURE 55 - COLLARS

BIBLIOGRAPHY

Erwin, Mabel D., *Practical Dress Design* (New York: The Macmillan
    Company, 1954).
Hillhouse, Marion S. and Evelyn A. Mansfield, *Dress Design* (Boston:
    Houghton-Mifflin, 1948).
Hollen, Norma, *Flat Pattern Methods* (Minneapolis: Burgess Publishing
    Company, 1961).

Unit Seven
Necklines

The face should be the center of interest at all times. All parts of the costume must combine to make this true. The texture of the fabric, the color, as well as line should all combine to make this the principal area of focus.

This is true of a garment whether or not it has a collar, but for a collarless one it is especially important. The natural beauty of the individual should be emphasized, and the less attractive features should have attention drawn away from them.

The oval shaped face is considered the most desirable. All faces do not have this shape, but through correct use of transition lines and optical illusion, the resulting effect may seem nearer the ideal. Lines that repeat a poor contour or feature emphasize it, as do lines that are in direct opposition. The latter tend to intensify the fault by creating a strong contrast. Harsh, geometric lines accentuate irregularities.

Lines should be softened through use of shapes harmonious with body contour, through use of suitable fabrics, and through careful consideration of proportions of the neckline. Geometric lines that are very harsh and have no relation to body contour should be avoided. One needs to develop judgment in the selection of fabrics and to understand the effect produced by different types of hand. (See Unit Nine.) As in all designing, the neckline must be considered in relation to its proportion, to the face, neck, hairline and head of the wearer, as well as to the whole design.

Lines that are U-shaped are soft in effect and V-shaped necklines are more flattering than harsher geometric lines. These two shapes can be manipulated to seemingly add width or length to the face and to the neck.

The face which is too slender can be made to seem broader by directing the eye in a horizontal direction. A neckline with a broadened U, one lowered at the center front, one square in effect but with a softened line, a bateau, a sweetheart neckline, all these can make the face seem broader. A U-neckline can be used for the slender face if the width of the U is greater than its depth.

The face with too much breadth needs an opposite type of treatment. Such a face can appear narrower through emphasis of vertical lines. The deeper and less wide the U or the V, the more length the face appears to have and, consequently, the more slender it seems. A square, angular jaw needs the same treatment but with more emphasis on the softening effect.

The thin face is often accompanied by a long thin neck. This too needs special attention. High necklines and rounded ones are usually becoming, especially if they are treated with a soft drape, by a smooth roll of the collar, or by a scarf. A cowl neck which covers part of the lower neck is good to make the neck seem shorter. A turtle neck collar, if not fitted too high and tight, is also helpful.

The thick neck requires the opposite treatment. A neckline which fits closely at the sides and then drops below the base of the neck is flattering. The longer the U or V, the more slender the neck seems.

Another troublesome type of neck is the one which is short. Many collars on a short neck give the appearance of the head sitting on the shoulders. The lesson to be learned from this is that it is better to have no collar or, at most, a small, flat one. The short neck appears longer with a neckline shaped slightly wider and then tapered inwardly as it drops below the base of the neck.

A surplice blouse should be mentioned in connection with necklines because of its versatility. Its asymetric design with the V-shaped neckline offers many possibilities to the designer. (See Figure 59d.)

In the following figures the collars are classified as the garments were in the introduction - tailored, semi-tailored, and dressy. To these three classifications another has been added for necklines - casual. The sketches found on the figures will be discussed in relation to the draping methods presented earlier. Further sketches will be added if they are needed to clarify the rendering of some designs.

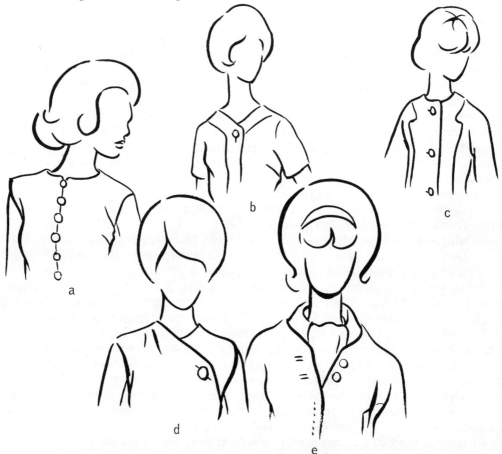

FIGURE 56 - NECKLINES FOR TAILORED GARMENTS

There will be some overlapping of the designs since there is no sharp line of demarkation. The fabric used, the accessorizing, and the wearer will all effect the classification of these necklines.

FIGURE 56

Figure 56 shows plain necklines good for tailored garments. Views a, b, and e show long slender necks which have been made to appear less long. View a shows a neckline which has been widened, but which has remained near the height of the basic dress in center front. In b the neckline is lowered and widened more than in a and the facings are used on the right side to give a diagonal line thus making the space seem broader. View e has used the softening effect of a scarf inside the lowered neckline.

View c has used a slightly lowered, round neckline. A small sheer scarf would soften this so it would be more becoming to many women and girls.

View d would be good for a thick neck because the neckline runs rather high on the sides and then drops below normal at center front. In fact it could be even lower and be more slenderizing.

FIGURE 57

Various types of necklines for semi-tailored garments are shown in Figure 57. These are softer in line and feel than those in Figure 56. View a of Figure 57 is a variation of a high loose cowl neck with a tie looped through a buttonhole to hold the cowl centered at the neck. The soft drape at the neck and the horizontal effect achieved through the halter treatment give an unusual neckline. It is not one to be worn on a short neck. Figure 60a shows how it will appear after draping.

View b is a simple neckline which has added interest through the slits on the raglan sleeve line and the stitching around the neckline. The round neckline would be a poor choice for one with a full face.

The neckline of c is lower on the sides than b and has part of the basic dart thrown into darts radiating at the neckline. This design should not be chosen unless the individual has an attractive neck.

View d is quite individual in its designing and would be especially suitable to older women. View d would be becoming with a rather round face as the deep V would give length. (See Figure 58 for details of draping.)

Figures 57 and 59 show several variations of the cowl and draped neckline. In Figure 59, view a is a high cowl which would be becoming to a long slender neck and slender face. View c shows a cowl which comes a little higher at the sides of the neck but lower and with more drape in the center front. View e shows a deep cowl which would probably need to be weighted in the center front to make it stay down in these folds. (A small plastic button could be used as the weight and hung on a swing tack.) Of these three cowl necklines the first would likely be more comfortable to wear. The cowl stops at the yoke line which results in the blouse staying in place better than when the whole blouse front is on the bias. Figure 60, b, c, and d respectively, shows how these three designs will appear after draping.

Views b and d, Figure 59, are versions of the surplice blouse. View b drapes high on the neck in front as the back also would do. (Note this surplice blouse could be interpreted in another manner, namely, with a shawl collar. (See Figure 53.) This high neckline would be becoming to a slender neck.

View d which is lower at center front than view b would be becoming to a thicker neck, especially if it were a little higher on the sides.

FIGURE 57 - NECKLINES FOR SEMI-TAILORED GARMENTS

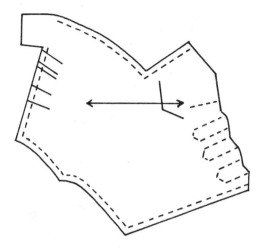

FIGURE 58 - DRAPING BLOUSE d, FIGURE 57

FIGURE 61

Figure 61 gives a variety of necklines ideas.   View a has a deep yoke with a high, fitted neckline which hugs the neck, both back and front.   The blouse front and raglan sleeves are gathered onto the yoke.   View b has a neckline which is wide at the sides but only slightly below the basic line in front.   The neck facing, which is on the outside, is pleasingly shaped.   View c gives a kimono blouse with the neckline in both back and front coming up higher than usual but lower on the sides.

The fabric used would determine whether or not the jacket in d is dressy or semi-dressy.   The design made in a brocade, for example, would result in a dressy garment.   The lowered, round neckline lends itself to multiple strands of beads.

A cascade of bias-cut ruffles outlines the center front band of view e and circles the neck under the edge of a fitted facing.

FIGURE 62

Sketches in Figure 62 (and 63) present ideas for necklines in dressy garments.   The wedding dress shows charm and youth in a low cut, scalloped neckline.   View d uses the scalloped treatment in a more sophisticated manner on the low cut blouse back.   Views b and e would both have outlining of the neckline on the dress form as initial steps in draping.   View b has the basic dart converted into the diagonal darts radiating from the waistline. View e is a variation of a French dart design.

View c shows a gracefully draped blouse front which would be cut on the bias.   The lower part of the blouse should be on the true bias.   The basic dart becomes the diagonal darts at left shoulder.

FIGURE 59 - NECKLINES FOR SEMI-TAILORED

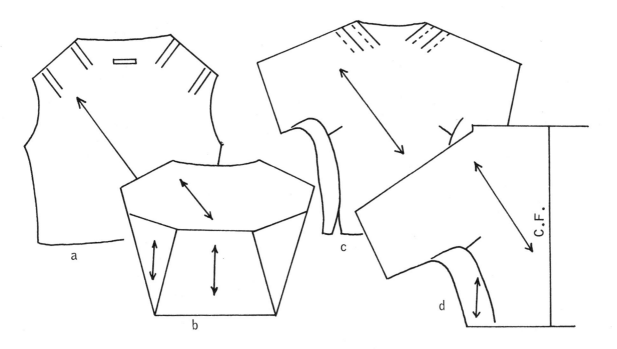

FIGURE 60 - INTERPRETATION OF SKETCHES ON FIGURE 57 AND 59

FIGURE 63 AND 64

View a, Figure 63, has been developed by draping which leads from the right side blouse up over the bustline on the left side. Sheered fabric forms the "modesty" in the center front V. A fabric similar to crepe would be necessary to achieve this effect while view b would need a fabric with more body.

View f is another version of the cowl neck. (See Figure 60.) Note what a variety of effects is obtained through the different ways of draping the cowl neck and through the contrast in hand of fabric used to obtain these effects. (See Figures 57a, 59a, c, and e, 63b, and f, 64c, d, and e.)

View c shows the blouse back forming the upper part of the blouse front. The lower blouse front sends tuck-darts into the shoulder yoke.

View d is another surplice but made with deep diagonal tucks, similar to Gibson girl tucks, at the shoulders.

View e is derived from a raglan one-piece sleeve. The center front section is full and gives the appearance of having the fullness held in place by the band which ends in loops at one side of the blouse front section.

How would the necklines in Figure 64b and f be developed?

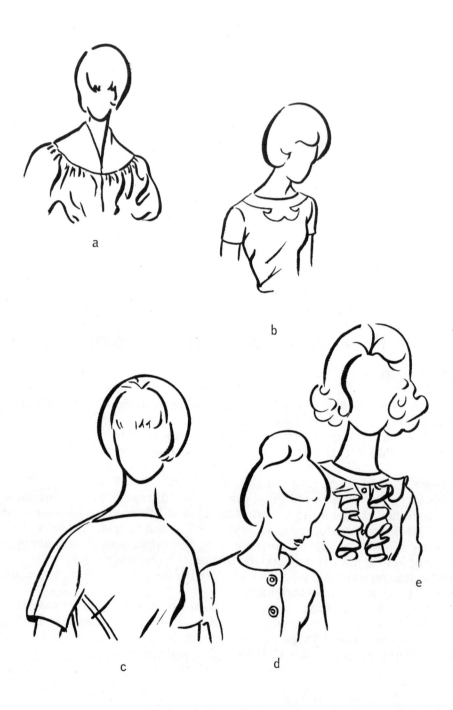

FIGURE 61 - NECKLINES FOR SEMI-TAILORED GARMENTS

FIGURE 62 - NECKLINES FOR DRESSY GARMENTS

FIGURE 65

In this figure all the necklines are casual, yet there is not one that could not become dressy or semi-tailored if the fabric were suitable.

View <u>a</u> shows a slightly lowered neckline which is faced back on the right side with braid accenting the edge of the contrasting fabric. Worn with the pants it is definitely casual.

The suntan dress, view <u>b</u>, has a yoke cut on the bias and gathered at the neckline by a cording which runs through a casing at the top of blouse front.

View <u>c</u> may be interpreted as a plain neck blouse topped with a kerchief tied in back or as a blouse with a cowl draped area.

A double fold ruffle on the straight of the fabric trims the round, lowered neckline found in view <u>d</u>.

View <u>e</u> is simple neckline cut low on the sides and at the center front. It is then faced on the right side in bias cut of self material.

Choose necklines with great care. Emphasize your good features. Use optical illusion and counter attractions to detract from poor features.

FIGURE 63 - NECKLINES FOR DRESSY GARMENTS

FIGURE 64 - NECKLINES

FIGURE 65 - NECKLINES FOR CASUAL GARMENTS

BIBLIOGRAPHY

Brockman, Helen L., *The Theory of Fashion Design*, (New York: John Wiley and Sons, Inc., 1965).

Chambers, Helen G., and Moulton, Verna, *Clothing Selection*, (New York: J. B. Lippincott and Company, 1961).

Cotton, Emmi, *Clothes Make Magic*, (New York: E. P. Dutton and Co., 1949).

Erwin, Mabel D., *Practical Dress Design*, (New York: Macmillan Company, 1954).

McJimsey, Harriet T., *Art in Clothing Selection*, (New York: Harper and Row, 1963).

Morton, Grace, *The Arts of Costume and Personal Appearance* (New York: John Wiley and Sons, Inc., 1964).

Ryan, Mildred G., and Phillips, Verna, *Clothes for You* (New York: Appleton-Century Company, 1939).

Unit Eight
Designing Dresses and Special Features

The preceeding units have dealt with the use of the dress form for learning the fundamentals of designing parts of a costume - the blouse, the skirt, the sleeve, the collar, and the neckline. To make a complete artistic costume all parts must be combined in relation to each other. There must be unity. (See Principles of Art, in Unit Nine.) This all important unity must have interesting composition which results from the imaginative use of guidelines learned for designing.

The reader has been given the techniques - the tools with which to work (with one exception which will be included in this unit). Her degree of success in producing fashion-right styles for herself will be limited only by her zeal and determination to apply her learnings.

This unit is organized in problems dealing with the placement of the waistline seam, or lack of it, in relation to the overall appearance of the dress, and features for added interest. Many sketches are shown. Some may give the reader ideas from which to develop a garment or to spark the imagination. Some of the sketches are discussed; others are for analysis and criticism. One problem, "Features for Interest" is presented with no comment. Study these well. Details of design and perfection of workmanship often make the difference between mediocrity and individuality in a garment.

Problem I: Dresses Without Waistline Seams

The straight dresses with no waistline seams have been very popular. They are fashionable and smart on those without many curves; they are dangerous for those with figure problems and weight. They reveal all and hide nothing in relation to the figure. Use caution in selecting them.

The designs illustrated in Figure 66 are severe in line and poor choices for many figures. The addition of a belt as in sketches c and e helps to relieve the severity but not enough for a person with "unfortunate bulges." The sketches a and b have unusual features which add interest--the button treatment on one and the open-side shift on the other. Are there unusual features on the other sketch?

Figure 67 also features dress without waistline seams, but all these have the severity reduced by flaring silhouettes, by emphasis on princess lines (design on the French dart line), by pleats, and by unusual treatment of pockets, button-and-buttonholes, and belts.

Would the dress on the left be more pleasing without the pocket at the yoke line? Would larger pockets of the same design be a good addition to the hip area?

FIGURE 66 - DRESSES WITHOUT WAISTLINE SEAM

FIGURE 67 - DRESSES WITHOUT WAISTLINE SEAMS

Consider the sketches in Figure 66. The method of procedure for draping dresses without waistlines, called sheaths, is presented below. This procedure can be followed to develop any of the sketches in Figure 66 as well as ones of individual design.

A. BASIC SHEATH

FRONT

Note: No opening has been planned for this type of dress. It will be necessary for the worker to plan this at the beginning of her work.

PREPARING THE FABRIC

1. Measure the length of the dress desired - from the side neck to the bottom of the skirt. Add 3" for the hem and 1" for the shoulder seam.
2. Measure the width of the largest part of the hips from side seamline to side seamline. Add 3/4" for ease (minimum on a straight sheath as it must fit snugly) and 2" for the side seams.
3. Measure the width of the bust from underarm seam to underarm seam. Add 2" for ease plus 2" for the side seam.
4. Use #2 or #3, whichever is the larger, for the width of fabric.
5. Tear the muslin by the length in #1 and the width in #4.
6. Straighten the fabric, mark the grainline and the center.
7. Shape the neck as wanted.

DRAPING THE FABRIC

(See Figure 68. On this drawing the fabric is shown folded so the markings on dress form can be seen; you should work with the fabric un-folded. The same is true with the sheath you are now draping.)
1. Place the center front of the fabric at the center front of the dress form, and pin from the neck through the hip area.
2. Pin the neck and shoulder seams; straighten the crosswise grainline through the bustline.
3. Pin the ease tucks at the bust and hip lines.
4. Pin the armhole.
5. Straighten the crosswise grain at the hipline, and pin to the dress form.
6. Make the underarm dart sufficient to take in all excess caused by straight-ening the grainline at the hips. Point the dart to the tip of the breast.
7. Pin the vertical dart in the midriff and hip areas.
8. Pin the side seam beginning at the hip and work up. Curve in the amount desired at waistline.
9. At the lower edge of the skirt turn under 1" for the side seam and pin.
10. Fold the fabric under from this point to the hip taking care to not stretch the fabric. Examine the effect. Decrease the fullness if desired.

11. Mark the lower edge of the hem allowance. It will probably run up on the grainline at the side 1/2" to 3/4".
12. Do not remove from the dress form at this time.
13. Repeat #1- #12 for the other side of the dress.

If the body is perfectly symmetrical, the second side can be a copy of the first. Many figures require draping each side.

BACK

PREPARING THE FABRIC

Prepare the fabric as for the front of the sheath.

DRAPING THE FABRIC

1. Unfold the fabric and pin the center back on the center back of the dress form from the neckline to the top of the midriff.
2. Pin the neck and the shoulder seams with the crosswise grain parallel to the floor in the width of the back area after making shoulder dart or ease.
3. Pin the ease-tucks at the bust and hip lines.
4. Pin the armhole.
5. Pin the center back below the waistline to the hip level. Note that this is not pinned in center back from #1 above until now. The fabric should not curve in at the center back.
6. Straighten the crosswise grain at the hipline, and pin it to the dress form.
7. Make the vertical dart.
8. Pin the side seam to the front side seam. There will be a little ease on the front seam line in the hip-to-waistline area. This will help overcome the swinging forward of the side seam. *NOTE:* On a straight, undarted sheath, a better fit can be obtained by making a diagonal underarm dart that originates slightly below the waistline than by using a higher dart.
9. Repeat for the second side of the dress form, if the sides of the figure are not matching.
10. Mark the notches along the side seams.
11. Remove both the back and the front. Mark the notches, seam lines, seam allowances, and darts.
12. Baste and fit.

B. PRINCESS DRESSES

FRONT

Outline on the dress form the lines for the princess dress, both the back and front, from the shoulders to the hipline; also for the neckline if it is not the normal line. Decide the width at the lower edge of the hem for the back, the front, and each gore. (See Figures 66e and 67b.)

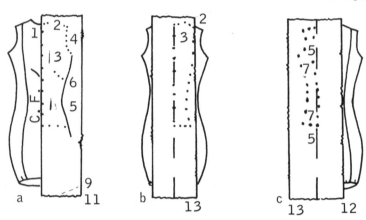

FIGURE 68 - PRINCESS DRESS

Note: In view a the numbers refer to instructions on pages 112 and 113, Draping the Fabric.

In views b and c the numbers refer to instructions on page 113.

PREPARING THE FABRIC (See Figure 68b)

1. Measure from the side neck to the length of the dress desired.
2. Measure from the beginning of the princess line (French dart line or variation) to the desired length of the dress.
3. Measure the center front panel at the bustline. Add 1 1/4" for the seams.
4. Determine the width of the center front panel at the bottom of the skirt after consideration of the amount of flare and seam allowances.
5. Repeat #4 for the side panels.
6. Cut the center front panel by the dimensions found in #1 and either #3 or #4 using the larger.
7. Cut two panels for the side front using measurements found in #2 and #5.
8. Straighten the fabric. Mark the grainlines and the center of the panel.
9. Cut the neckline in accordance with the design.

DRAPING THE FABRIC

1. Pin the center front panel at the center front of the dress form from the shoulder to the hipline. (See Figure 68b.) Leave 1" seam allowance at the shoulder.
2. Pin the neckline and the shoulder seam as far as the princess line is marked on the dress form.
3. Pin to the dress form following the design lines - extending from the top of the design line to below the waistline 4" or 5". Leave this while working on the side panels. Repeat for second side of center panel.
4. Place the side panel on the dress form so that the center runs at right angles to the floor in a position slightly nearer the side seam than the front of the panel. (See Figure 68c.)

5.   Pin the hip and midriff areas on the warpwise grainline.
6.   Smooth the fabric through the shoulder and bust areas and pin at the
     shoulder line. The crosswise grainline will not be parallel to the floor in
     the armhole area.
7.   Pin ease-tucks at the bustline (nearer the side seam than usual) and the
     hipline.
8.   Pin the armhole.
9.   Pin the front seam of the panel down 4" or 5" below the waistline as in
     #3 above. Ease the fabric in over the bustline. If the design line does
     not run over the bustline, read in Unit Four, page 42.
10. Pin the underarm seams down 4" or 5" below the waistline as in #3 and
     #9 above. Curve in the seam at the waistline according to the design.
11. Repeat #4-#10 for the second side panel, if needed.
12. Work on the seams, now, where the side and center front panels meet.
13. Turn under the normal seam allowance on each seam at the bottom of the
     skirt and pin together in touching points.
14. Examine the hang of the skirt as to the origin of flare at the hip line and
     the fullness at the hip and lower edge.
15. Make any desired changes.
16. Leave it on the dress form while the back is being draped.

BACK

PREPARING THE FABRIC

Prepare the fabric as for the dress front.

DRAPING THE FABRIC

The fabric will be draped by the same directions as the front. The only
variation is that there will be less fabric eased in over the shoulder blades
than over the bustline.
1.   When ready to pin the side seams pin them to the front side seams. The
     front seam in the hip-to-waistline area will be eased in slightly onto the
     back seam.
2.   Mark all seamlines, seam allowances, and darts, if any.
3.   Mark the cutting edge of the hem.
4.   Cut, baste, and fit.

Problem II: Dresses With Waistline Seams

Figures 69, 70, and 71 show dresses with waistline seams. The waistline treatment is a perennial favorite, always good but not always high fashion.
The more garments conform to the normal body lines and contours, the more
pleasing they will be to the majority of people.

FIGURE 69 - DRESSES WITH WAISTLINE SEAM

FIGURE 70 - DRESSES WITH WAISTLINE SEAMS

Figure 69 presents tubular skirts which are worn best by those with slim figures. Each of these is basically a simple dress, but, even so, each is outstanding in some way. Notice that in each of these the outstanding features have become a part of the construction lines. Through the skillful use of stitching, cording, stripes, tucks, tabs, simulated overblouse, or peplum each of the designs is a little different, is individual.

Figure 70 shows waistline treatments completely different from those in Figure 69 — except the center one. View a is a little difficult to classify, as it is a diagonal line beginning low on the right and running to a high level on the left side. The gathering into the bias line belt is a little surprising in itself, due to the manner in which the gathering ends before it reaches the side seam at the right side. An element of surprise in design is good.

The long formal, e, has little to recommend it but its simplicity and harmony of fabric, design, and figure. It could be referred to as a classic. The fabric would probably be the feature that would make this successful or mediocre.

Gathers are used skillfully to take the place of the basic dart in the blouse front of view c. More fullness has been added to the basic skirt to give it the needed fullness for the gathering. The hand of the fabric would determine how much fullness needs to be added. In a light weight fabric much fullness would be needed to give this effect. It would give the skirt a peg-top shape, that is, larger at the top than at the bottom. The twisted belt of self material is a good finishing note.

Tiers of tucks in view d are developed in the blouse front and would carry on to the back. They end with the lowest one covering the waistline. The ease at the skirt top is gathered at the side front to give a well-proportioned division of areas in the skirt front.

The remaining garment on this page, view e, has a slight blouson effect.* The skirt is fitted snugly through the hip area but has much fullness beginning at this line. This fullness is produced by the insertion of godet pleats at the seam lines.

Figure 71 is made up of one-piece dresses with the waistline seam in normal position, but each frock has a flaring skirt. The two on the left are dressy garments. View a has achieved distinction through the skillful combination of fabrics and through strong transitional lines leading from the radiating pleats of the skirt into the blouse. View b is a soft, very feminine design with fullness developed in the top of the flared skirt, into the waistline, and into the line of the raglan sleeve. The tailored band at neck with a matching effect worked into the tie-belt gives a finished look to the composition.

The two garments on the right are very much alike in silhouette. View d has radiating pleats which emphasize the silhouette while view c has stitching on the seam lines which gives emphasis to the dart treatment in the blouse and in the center front. The back of view d repeats the lines of the dress front.

*See #5, page 60.

FIGURE 71 - DRESSES WITH WAISTLINES

Problem III: Dresses With High Waistline Seams

The high waistline seam intermittently returns to favor. Figure 95 gives a modern version of a high waistline of the *Directoire* period. The frocks in Figure 72 are less dressy than the one in Figure 93 and show great variation in the treatment of the above-normal waistline.

In design a the inset midriff gives both an above and a below normal line. The gathering in the blouse and skirt in corresponding areas gives a unity that could be a little monotonous, if it were not for the shape of the inset.

Sketches b and c are somewhat alike in treatment but not in details of the allocation of the basic dart. The lowered neckline and turtle-neck collar on dress c give a feeling of completeness to the design which is somewhat lacking in view b. The waistline in d runs from normal in center front to high at the dart on the French dart line and probably continues high across the back. This would be pleasing for a mature figure if the individual has a flat stomach.

The effect of a princess line is given in view e which has a waistline in center front only. The radiating pleats give gracefulness to the skirt.

The last figure on the page, f, combines a graceful draped cowl neckline with large pressed tucks running from the off-shoulder position to the high waistline. Note that the ease over the bustline is placed on the center panel because of the location of the diagonal shoulder pleats. (See discussion, page 42.)

Problem IV: Dresses With Low Waistline Seams

Proportion must be given special attention in a dress with a low waistline seam. This is particularly true in a period of shor skirts.

The sketches in Figure 73 show five completely different designs with the waistline seam below normal. Sketches a, b, and c are the ones most likely to give problems. The upper part of the garment should be shorter than the skirt area if both proportion and balance are observed. If a short person, who wears equally short skirts, tries one of these, the dress will likely have an uninteresting half and half proportion, or the blouse will be longer than the skirt.

Sketches d and e are better for the individual who is under 5'4" because the blouse is high hip length leaving a skirt longer than the blouse.

Problem V: Two-Piece Dresses

The same caution is needed for two-piece dresses as for low-waistline garments - observe proportion. Are the parts related to each other and to the whole? Sketch a, Figure 74, introduces a third part, the yoke, which is topped with a version of the turtle collar. The whole figure must be considered in relation to these four parts as well as to the length of the skirt.

FIGURE 72 - DRESSES WITH HIGH WAISTLINE SEAMS

FIGURE 73 - DRESSES WITH LOW WAISTLINE

FIGURE 74 - TWO-PIECE DRESSES

FIGURE 75 - TWO-PIECE DRESSES

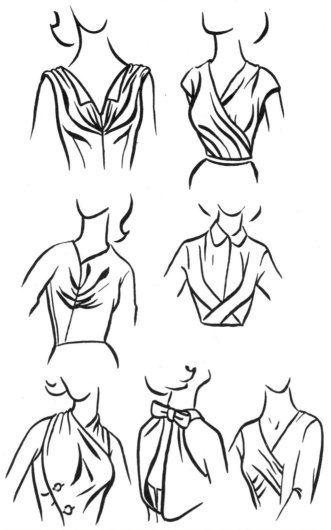

FIGURE 76 - DRAPING IN THE BLOUSE AREA

Views b, c, and e, of Figure 74 could easily develop into half-and-half proportions with the top the same length as the visible portion of the skirt.   This
proportion is uninteresting and monotonous.   Sketch d would be the best
choice for a petite figure.

    The neck treatment in view b is different from any presented up to this
point.   It is achieved by curving the shoulder seam up rather than by hugging
the shoulder.   Careful choice of interfacing is essential to assure that the
neckline will remain standing at the side neck.   (Note the neckline of sketch
c.)

    The skirt top of the two-piece dress may have a band, may have a fitted
facing which is stiffly interlined, or it may be on a camisole top.

    The figures in Figure 75 require the same consideration concerning
proportion.   Sketch a needs thorough analysis of the shoulder line before it

is chosen.   The low rounded yoke could make one appear very round should-
ered if she is not erect and could also make the shoulders seem very wide.
Sketch c offers good opportunity for texture and color contrasts if the proportions are pleasing.

What features in Figure 75e, b, and d add to the attractiveness? Which
detract?

Problem VI: Features for Interest

Figure 76 shows a variety of ways to drape a blouse.   Each one would
be challenging to drape.   Although the directions are not given for these
specific designs, the techniques which should give the reader all the needed
guidance have been presented.   Experiment!

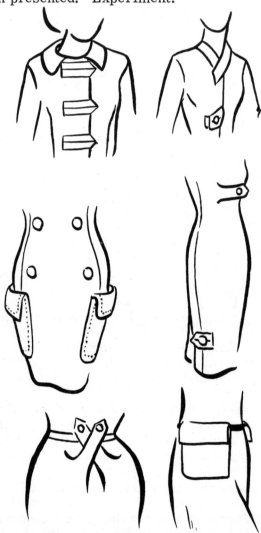

FIGURE 77 - POCKETS AND TABS

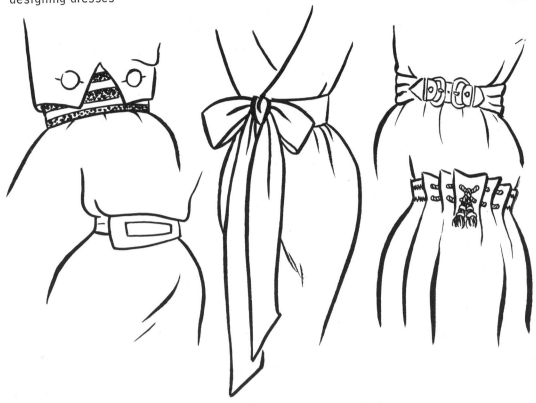

FIGURE 78 - BELTS AND BUCKLES AND BOWS

Figure 77 presents rather conservative, tailored lines. Tabs or pockets of matching or contrasting fabric can be made in many different ways. (See also Figure 74d.)

See Figure 74 and Figure 69 for criticism.

Variations in belts offer opportunity to the person with imagination. Figure 78 presents a few. Make a collection of ideas for belts and waistline treatments.

Look through your file of clippings. (See page 136, Unit Nine.) How many unusual suggestions did you find? On what ones can you improve?

BIBLIOGRAPHY

Cotton, Emmi, *Clothes Make Magic*, (New York: E. P. Dutton and Company, 1949).

Erwin, Mabel, *Practical Dress Design*, (New York: The Macmillan Company, 1954).

Gutherie, Mary E., and Leite, Viletta, and Ericson, June, *The Arts of Costume and Personal Appearance*, (New York: John Wiley and Sons, Inc., 1964).

Hillhouse, Marion S. and Mansfield, Evelyn A., *Dress Design* (Boston: Houghton-Mifflin Company, 1948).

Unit Nine
Designing for the Individual

Clothing Appeal

What does a woman want from her clothing? One person might answer
quickly, "Comfort"; another, "Fashion"; or still another, "Enhancement."
There are many possible responses. Another, after pondering a little, might
decide she could not answer this question in one word, realizing that what
women want is very complex and is the result of many considerations. No
two people are interested in clothing in exactly the same way, yet practically
everyone is interested in dress.

Clothing has a universal appeal which began among primitive peoples.
Psychologists, anthropologists, and sociologists have theorized about the
origins of clothing. Of the many ideas suggested, two of the strongest are
that clothes were first worn for protection and decoration. In a beginning
society protection may have been the primary notive. Decorations soon became just as important to the developing culture. The increasing desire to
compete with others, to set oneself apart from others (yet remain one of the
group), and to attract attention (especially that of the opposite sex) spurred
individuals to increase the use of self-decoration. Decoration in time became
a symbol of status; during the centuries it changed in form but never in
meaning. In primitive cultures the number of snake rattlers or rings a man
wore around his neck, or the certain type of feathers he wore in his headdress
were a few of the decorations used to distinguish him from the masses. As
Western civilization developed status was revealed by the wearer's long
pointed shoes, sleeves slit to reveal linen underwear, long trailing gowns,
the use of purple, sleeves that dragged on the ground, and many, many other
such symbols. As Meshke summarizes, "...Apparel soon reflected the
psychological and sociological involvements which give rise to competition and
jealousy and which symbolize status, power and authority."[1]

What symbols of status can be seen on your campus? In a rural community? In an urban community?

Influence of the Social Order

Since everyone has his own approach to life, each has different wants
and values. "Values grow out of human interests and desires."[2] These values,
although individual, have developed from forces exerted by man's society and
particularly by his own segment of this society, his home. The impact of
one's social group is very important in the development of his standards,

values, and behavior. As Ryan says, "Knowledge of social psychological aspects of clothing is, therefore, basic to the study of clothing."[3]

Dressing in keeping with the standards of one's group helps one to be accepted and to develop his personality. Each person needs group approval. Rosencranz states that one of the appeals of clothing is "...the great dependency which we have upon one another for emotional support and personality integration."[4] The way a person acts and the role he plays are largely affected by his clothing. Ryan says, "Clothing serves in the main a social purpose just as food serves in the main a health purpose."[5] Not only is appropriate clothing a social asset, it has also become a requirement of the business world. Clothing, along with other possessions, is a very definite symbol of success or lack of it.

In this cultural period in the United States one has many casual acquaintances. First impressions are very important. Not only has clothing taken on added significance, but also has grooming--one's own body treatment. Good grooming increases the effectiveness of one's clothing and is so much a part of one's appearance that it has become an important consideration. Dorsey has found a high relationship between ratings in clothing, grooming, and poise.[6] There is never a time when one can be careless in the attention given to her grooming.

The home interprets the emphasis culture places on clothing and, "...determines, to a large extent, the attitudes and ideas, the prejudices and emotional feelings of its members."[7] The family's attitude will influence the importance the individual places upon clothing, the degree to which he conforms to the accepted standards of a group, and his concern over being a part of the community. This attitude will determine his personal emphasis of the various aspects of clothing—the aesthetic, the practical, and the creative.

It is true that in this century many outside influences have been felt— television; movies; radio; the printed media, such as newspapers, magazines, and literature; and the like. However, the family group in the American culture is the interpreter of society. The individual, then, develops from the family interpretation his own particular set of values.

Standards of dress vary from one part of this country to another. Indeed, differences are obvious among small groups within a large population. Importance of dress, however, differs little. In this period of rapid transportation of products and ideas, and of the development of the ready-to-wear industry, which is producing new fashions to fit different income levels, the difference in standards between groups is diminishing.

Emotional feelings of the individual, role playing, and group approval have been mentioned above in connection with the importance of clothing. The relation of clothing to self-concept is also of significance. All clothes evoke some degree of ego involvement on the part of the wearer.[8] Clothes are good or right for him only if they are helpful in building, rather than destroying, his possibilities, if they may "function to strengthen weak body image,"[9] to raise self esteem, to extend one's person. Clothing, correct in the individual's mind, makes role playing easier, facilitates seeking group acceptance. "We have no norms, or standards, for choice of clothing comparable to nutritional standards for food."[10] Hence, the person must learn how to express himself, to present his self-concept, to show his individuality yet

remain within the unwritten standards of his society. (In later pages wardrobe selection will be developed further.)

The woman who wishes to be well dressed is especially fortunate in
today's economy in two ways: she is living in an affluent age, and she is
living in an age of phenomenal developments within the fashion industry. Increased incomes have made it possible for the family to spend more than
ever before for clothing. The ready-to-wear industry caters fashion-right
garments for all incomes above subsistence levels, and the home sewer has
commercial patterns and fabrics in a wide variety of qualities, textures, and
designs. Though the family can spend more for clothing, studies show that
actually a lower per cent of the family income is being spent for clothing;
that clothing is having to compete with other items which are also status symbols. Oppenheim found that in 1947-49 the per cent of the disposable income
allocated to clothing was 12.6, whereas in 1963 it was 8.7 per cent.[11] Though
the family values will determine what part of this income can be used for
clothing, the development of a mutual clothing concept, planning, and good
management within the group take time and patience.

The Impact of Fashion

Until recent years fashion was considered by many people to be merely
the result of women's fickle tastes, their desires for change, their means
for competing with other women, and their devices for attracting the opposite
sex. There is an element of truth here, but underneath there are other
strong factors, in addition to big business, that cannot be ignored. Though
social scientists, in varying degrees, recognize that clothing is a strong
socio-psychological force, they have done little research in this area. However, home economists have shown considerable interest in the relation of
the behavioral aspects of people and their clothing. A growing number of
studies are developing.

Fashion is an outgrowth of the spirit of the period. The dress of people
reflects their culture. "The social order exists through time. Change
occurs in the cultural pattern and its social organizations as individuals
react."[12] As Chambers points out, periods of intense ferment usually bring
periods of fantastic color and fashion changes, whereas in a static society
mode of dress may vary only slightly over long periods.[13] (Is the spirit of
today related to the dress of today?)

Since the life of the Western World is in a state of flux, fashion also is
in a state of constant change. Fashion change, although continual, is gradual.
Kroeber presents the theory that in this gradual change there has been a
cycle running from short to long skirts in a period approximately one hundred
years long.[14] Agnes Young in *Recurring Cycles of Fashion* deals with this
theory of cycles in relation to silhouettes, which she classifies as tubular,
bell-shaped, and full-backed.[15] Each of these writers has series of pictures
illustrating his own theories. (Is there one silhouette prevalent today?)

The social structure of the Western World has changed greatly and
rapidly in this century. This change has been reflected in the current fashions

which have changed more rapidly than at any other time in history. This change in fashion has resulted from the social state, as well as from scientific advancement and the development of technology.

Especially after World War I (when women began to have more freedom in social and political affairs, in activity outside the home, and in business) there was a great change in dress. The explanation was that if women were to be this active, clothing needed to be designed for the type of life they led. Greater simplicity was introduced; at first it often resulted in severe tailoring, unbecoming to most women. However, as women began to feel confident in their new freedom, fashions returned to more feminine details of dress. Clothing became more functional than before this period of greater freedom, but as McJimsey says, it was, "... still chosen for fashion and decoration. "[16] American dress has changed considerably from the time when clothing was either for dress or for work. [17] Though today's woman, who works away from home, needs clothing suitable for this work, she also needs other garments for dress, for work at home, for social life, and for relaxation.

"The most dramatic change in the past thirty years has been in the decreasing formality of American clothing. This decrease in formality reflects other changes in family life. "[18] The more casual manner of living, given impetus by the movement to suburbs, has brought the need for clothing for relaxation--casual clothing for casual living.

The popularity of casual dress has not lessened woman's interest in new fashions. She still wants the new. Cecil Beaton says people take up the new because of a secret need for change. [19]

Though the following classifications of dress were made by Paul Nystrom[20] in 1928, no one has improved on them:

> Style--that which has specific, distinguishing traits and
> characteristics;
> Fashion--that which is the prevailing style of any time;
> Mode--is a synonym for fashion;
> Fad--merely a miniature fashion in some important matter or
> detail, usually short lived.

Two present-day classifications can be added to these:

> High Style or High Fashion--that which is extreme in design and
> that has appeal to only a small group;
> Classic--those designs once in fashion but held on past their time
> because of their utility value.

One classification may appeal to one person and one to another. However, the wardrobe of each woman, who considers herself fashionably dressed, is probably made of all classifications—style, fashion, classic—except fads. Each woman who is a leader in dress has probably studied her own individuality to the point that she has her own individual style to which she adapts the classifications of dress and fashions rather than accepting them as they are.

Ryan in *Clothing: A Study in Human Behavior* used the term "cycle" in a different manner from that in which Young used it. She presents another important view of the longevity of fashion. She says, "It is true that at least some aspects of style do recur at various periods, but when we speak of fashion cycle we mean something different. It refers to the gradual rise and fall of a particular fashion. When a style is first introduced it is followed by

a few daring individuals. Presently their clothing is copied and the particular
fashion is adopted by those people who are considered 'smart' and 'fashionable'. Finally, it is accepted by large masses of people and the style thus
reaches its peak. When it has been accepted by the majority of people, then
those who were the first to adopt it, change to a new fashion and the wave
starts to drop off. "[21]

The woman who wishes to be well dressed, yet able to wear her clothing
for a number of years, must learn to catch a style at the start of its fashion
cycle rather than at its peak of popularity. To be successful in choosing at
the correct time, one must study trends which will forecast the future. This
study will lead to close watching of changes in style details; to careful reading
of news releases on fashion openings of the leading fashion houses in France,
Italy, and America; to giving faithful attention to the leading fashion magazines.

Self-Concept

A statement commonly heard and repeated says that there are no ugly
American women, and that there is no need for any women to be unattractive.
Emmi Cotton has given emphasis to this conclusion when she says, "Some
(women), of course, can never be pretty; but the woman does not exist who
can't look interesting. . . and an interesting looking woman can be as attractive
as a pretty one. "[22]

The 1930's saw the introduction of the idea that it was better to be smart
looking than pretty. [23] It is the fortunate person who can be both smart and
pretty, but the first is in one's own power to achieve. Today few woman want
to be merely pretty. "Like the creative artist, intelligent people see beauty
in what may have been considered homeliness in former days. . . We know that
real beauty comes from within. Surface prettiness is largely a transitory
attribute of the young; beauty is an ageless quality. "[24] The famous Dior
commented that women are the most fascinating after they are thirty-five.

A candid analysis of one's self is important—and difficult. An objective
attitude is necessary to make this analysis and concept of self as impersonal
as possible. Mary Ryan says, "The concept a person has of himself possess-
ing certain characteristics is an important determiner of his behavior or the
roles which he assumes."[25] An analysis of one's self will help in his choice
of clothing, in the selection of what is good for his physical self, and what is
good for him as an individual. It is important for him in taking his place in
society, for playing his role in life. Beauty cannot be built, but one can
achieve an illusion of it by improving his natural appearance. [26] The result
of this improvement should not give one a feeling of self-consciousness, but
should give him a feeling of relaxation and poise and an ability to forget himself in his interest of the moment.

Wardrobe Planning

It is not a simple task to build an adequate wardrobe. The many activities in a woman's life today require an increasing number of types of gar-

ments.   This type of wardrobe needs to be built slowly and with extreme care.
Only in this manner can an individual have a wardrobe that will not prompt
her to say on occasion, "I haven't a thing to wear." This planning requires
careful analysis of the present wardrobe before considering additions and
replacements. Chambers gives excellent advice when she expresses the idea
of keeping the wardrobe current. [27]

Another good rule is to keep a "working wardrobe." If garments are
not worn, they should be given to someone who can use them. Many women,
with closets filled with clothing, have numerous garments which they never
wear, but which they say they are keeping until they come back in style. That
fashions in clothes will be identically repeated is a false premise. Fashions
do not return in true form. Some detail or line may be revived but not the
fashion of the garment as a whole. A glance at the two following illustrations
(Figure 79) will show how the simple over-draped skirt of 1966 has brought
back a variation of the more elaborately draped skirt of 1930.

FIGURE 79

Another idea for developing a current, working wardrobe is stated, "If a garment hasn't been worn for a year, give it to someone who can use it before it is completely outmoded." A well-dressed woman does not wear garments that are outmoded. If the owner feels that she must wear them for a longer time because she has not received their value in wear, she is confessing that she has not planned well. She may have bought more during one season than she could use; she may have bought too late in the fashion cycle; or she may have bought a fad. Buying too late in a fashion cycle results from failure to study fashion trends well enough to avoid error in buying. This woman is the one who should learn from the statement, "The basis of a good small wardrobe is a balanced plan, one which includes an adequate variety and number of clothes for the varied activities of your life."[28] If she has studied trends of fashion, she will have garments which she can expect to wear for several years, and she will buy wisely before the peak of fashion.

A current, working wardrobe needs an added descriptive term— "individual". A wardrobe should be in keeping with the wearer's personal qualities which make her unique.

A garment from a rack in a department store, where there are possibly four matching models in varying sizes, is rather lacking in individuality. When it is on the wearer it takes on some of her personality. If she is clever, she adds effective touches in accessorizing a ready-made. If she is making a garment, she must apply this same cleverness in using the majority of commercial patterns. These two--accessorizing and redesigning a commercial pattern--supply splendid opportunities to use creativity and produce an outstanding wardrobe.

Another descriptive word for this current, working, individual wardrobe is "interesting". Give it a surprising element which may result from an amusing accessory, a challenging color combination, an unusual texture or texture combination, a novel construction detail, or some other product of your imagination.

A woman may think she does not have the ability to create or the courage to wear an individual and interesting wardrobe, although she admires this type of clothing on another. If she wants to make her wardrobe more attractive, she will begin with the self-analysis, choose her best physical traits and build upon them. Gradually she will find more self confidence which will be followed by more willingness to experiment. She will soon find that she can conform to her group standards and not lose her individuality because she has learned that, "The key to distinctive dressing lies in the relationship between the character of the woman and the character of her clothes."[29]

Four descriptive words have been used in relation to this ideal wardrobe—current, working, individual, and interesting. By what means will this wardrobe be achieved?

One means of producing a satisfactory wardrobe is to develop good taste. Good taste is not inborn; but whether or not one develops it is dependent upon environment, emotions, training or study, and observation. "Good taste in the field of art is the application of the principles of design to problems in life where appearance as well as utility is a consideration."[30] The principles and elements of art will be commented on briefly, only to remind the student

of them.   The students who are using this text have studied previously the
basis of art composition in other courses in home economics and art.   (There
are many excellent texts for studying art principles.   See Bibliography)
These principles are basic to good taste and the building of an interesting
wardrobe.

Good taste, according to Chambers and Moulton, implies proper use of
material, design, and color.[31]   Good taste should be a growing thing, a constant striving for new ideas and new applications of them.   Money is helpful
when building a wardrobe but not essential for one of good taste.   It should
be kept in mind that the ideal of good taste of a culture changes; hence, what
may be good at one time may be considered poor at another.

Application of art standards must be observed in apparel as well as in
other forms of artistic expression.   It must be admitted that there are times
in fashion (as has been true in earlier periods) when art standards are vio-
lated.   However, the individual wearer need not be guilty of following such
fashion.   The creative person can always adapt the fashion to her own standards and individuality.

No costume can be a work of art if unity is not observed.   Every part
and every detail must contribute to the oneness.   To make this a harmonious
whole, the principles of art--dominance, balance, proportion, and rhythm--
must be used as guides to develop the relation of the parts to the whole.
Interest must be maintained through these principles which are developed with
the proper use of the essential elements--line, form, color, and texture.
The human figure must be kept in mind as the basis for line and form.
Through correct use of line unbecoming bulges or body deformities may be
hidden or seem to take on new form through optical illusion.

Color has very strong appeal and is the element to which many people
react first.   Studies have shown a correlation between color choice and personality traits.   (See Bibliography.)   Color must be studied in relation to the
wearer--to her coloring, to other physical characteristics--as well as to its
effect on her personality.   Helen Chamber states that, "Color is a challenge;
it is fun; and it is a strong, dominating factor in your ultimate satisfaction
with how you look."[32]   Color is a subjective matter.   A woman's reaction to
it is based on her culture but is tempered by her own personality and values.

Maintaining a basic color scheme is another means to a successful
wardrobe.   A basic color scheme will have a predominant color to which all
else is keyed.   In the winter the coat usually sets the basic color.   This gives
a coordinated wardrobe in which parts belong to one another.   This wardrobe
can be achieved by interesting selections and combinations of values,
intensities, and textures.

Many well-dressed women have more than one basic color scheme.
They may have, for instance, one for fall-winter and one for spring-summer.
To have more than one basic color requires a more extensive wardrobe, at
least as far as accessories are concerned, and requires careful planning for
skillful coordination.

Texture, also, has a strong appeal and some people react to it before
color.[33]   This element must be given very careful attention in planning a
garment, for there must be close harmony between it, the design, and the

wearer.   The draping process gives the worker special appreciation of texture, since its characteristics determine to a great extent how the garment
will be designed.   Let it "talk to you. " (See Figure 80.)

A feeling for quality must be developed if one is to become a good judge
of workmanship, worth of the fabric, and selection of findings.

A wardrobe built on long range planning, self-analysis, application of
art criteria, and good taste needs another consideration—care. No wardrobe
can remain at its best if it is not properly cared for through proper cleaning,
pressing, and repairing. In fact, the care of a garment should be considered
at the time of purchase—method and cost of cleaning, dimensional stability,
durability of fabric and trim, and ease of soiling.

When one has learned to make an objective self-analysis, to choose
discriminatingly, to have the courage to keep that precious individuality while
remaining part of the group, she will find that she feels well-dressed, confident and poised. With this self-conficence she is better prepared to cope with
the problems of the day.

The wide variety of products on the market today makes decision making
difficult for the consumer. She needs to keep informed on fibers, finishes,
and construction methods. These increase in number each year, thus increasing the problem of decision making. She needs to know what she can
expect from the fibers and finishes and be able to read, interpret, and apply
the information given on garments and on bolts of piece goods. This is asking
much of the purchaser, "Yet if full value is to be received from the dollars
spent for clothing, some knowledge of quality of fabrics and the construction
of garments is necessary. "[34]

FIGURE 80 - "LISTENING" TO HER FABRIC

A Decision—To Buy or To Make

Production of ready-made clothing has become big business, especially in France and the United States. This development has resulted in a multiplicity of type and grade of garments, which further complicates the task of the buyer because there is so much from which to select. Soon after the inception of a fashion, it is available throughout the country at many price levels; this results in varying qualities of fabric and workmanship. It gives the shopper another complication of deciding about price in relation to quality. She must also judge fit, since many figures do not lend themselves to standard sizes. Alterations may be required. She must ask herself "Can this be made to fit properly?"

There are many points in favor of purchasing ready-made garments:
1. They may be seen in their final form.
2. Many fabrics in ready-to-wear garments are not available in piece goods.
3. Time is saved by buying rather than making.
4. Many findings and trimmings are available to the manufacturer but not to the home dressmaker.
5. Professional touches are given the garments.
6. More consumer information is available on ready-to-wear clothing than on bolts of fabrics.

For some individuals sewing is a highly rewarding, creative experience as discussed in the introduction. To such a person there are more advantages in making than in buying the finished product. However, there are a number of points she should consider before she decides to make a certain garment:
1. Can she plan and visualize the garment well enough to be satisfied when it is completed?
2. Does she have the necessary time?
3. Does she have the skill needed for the garment as planned?
4. Does she have the necessary equipment?
5. Can she find the fabric and findings of the quality, color, and texture desired?
6. Can she fit herself properly?
7. Is her motivation sufficient to make her give up other activities in favor of this?

"Every individual is a designer inasmuch as he puts together all components of the dress in one picture."[35] This is true, to a degree, in assembling the wardrobe from commercially-made garments, but it is even more so when a person makes the garments herself. To achieve a beautiful design she must have perfect coordination between all parts—the fabric, pattern, findings—and each must be beautiful in itself. A fine professional appearance cannot be produced from cheap material, careless workmanship and poor fit.

Decoration is often a weak point in garments made at home and in inexpensive bought garments. Decoration must be in character and obey the art principles.[36] Decoration must seem to be a part of the garment, not an after thought. A little decoration done subtly is better than lavish use of it. That which seems to be a structural part of the garment or to come from a structural part is usually more satisfying. (See discussion, page 116.)

A professional-appearing garment requires skill and patience, but if it is well done, the worker is rewarded by the quality of the finished product. Hand details giving an individuality can be added effectively by the skilled technician. Examples of such details are:

Smocking	Faggoting
Tranponto	Cording
Tucking	Lace
Chinese knots	Pick-stitching

Sources of Design

Draping can be a very satisfying, creative experience. With the non-professional designer the limitations are her own ability, her imagination, and the uses to be made of the garment. [37] It is usually wise to have an idea in mind to start with, but as the fabric is handled, it may be found that another design will suit the fabric better. Let the fabric have a chance to lead the way.

A FILE OF SKETCHES AND CLIPPINGS

Each woman who sews should have a file of sketches and clippings; collecting them as she finds details which appeal to her—a design of a collar, a cuff, a pleat treatment, a belt, to name a few. She should clip the picture, make a sketch or tracing of the idea, and file it away. Then when she is ready to plan a garment, she can look through her collection for ideas. The design, thus composed, will be more truly hers than one she copies or buys.

AWARENESS OF THE WORLD AROUND YOU

Few things that a person designs, or does, are wholly original. One has usually seen something or heard of something which has some effect on the design she makes. It may have been long ago that the inspiration was received and stored in the subconscious memory, or it may have been of recent origin. A combination of borrowed ideas from a variety of resources will result in a new design much more interesting to achieve, and much less likely to be seen on another, than a copy of even the best "original" design of a member of the Haute Couture. A design composed in this manner is much more one's own and is much more stimulating to the worker than a reproduction of the work of another person.

Many a woman hesitates to combine ideas in this way, because she lacks confidence in her own ideas and because copying one makes her feel more secure. She needs to try simple variations of fashion at first, such as a simple ornament that she adds; or a slight change of a commercial pattern. Then little by little she gains more confidence and eventually has the courage to design her own garments. She may be able to identify the source of some of the ideas, of others she may not. The latter may be original, or they may

FIGURE 81 - MODERN ADAPTATION
OF A SPANISH DESIGN

FIGURE 82

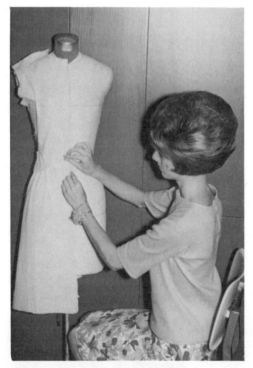

FIGURE 83

FIGURE 85

FIGURE 84

FIGURE 86 *

SOURCE AND DEVELOPMENT OF AN IDEA FOR A DESIGN

* Reproduced with permission from The Mood in Costume, by R. Turner Wilcox, Chas. Scribner's Sons, 1948.

FIGURE 87 *   FIGURE 88

be those of others which have long been stored in her mind for future use. However this may be, she will have the satisfaction of composing the whole which is a part of her and her personality.

She must open her eyes to the world around her. She will find inspiration from many unexpected sources; she may see something in nature which has an interesting arrangement of parts, striking color contrasts, or challenging texture combinations; she may observe interesting space treatments in architecture; she may be pleased by a belt on a passerby. She must *see all.*

HISTORIC DRESS AS A SOURCE OF IDEAS

Although it is true that fashions do return periodically, rarely— if ever —are they in exactly the same form. One may receive an idea from some period garment, but fashions interpret the age for which they are designed. Hence, the chosen design must be modified to fit the period of today, which stresses simplicity. One would probably never find a complete garment in historical design which she would want to wear except as a costume. However, one detail or one part of a frock might catch the imagination. Either could be fitted into today's silhouette and the designer could proceed from there with the idea.

*Reprinted with permission from Peasant Costume in Europe, Vol. II, by Kathleen Mann, A. & C. Black, Ltd., London, 1938.

Adapting historic design is one means of achieving distinction in clothing design—a modern adaptation of a very old design. It can result in a very beautiful, and satisfying, original design.

Examination of a few historic costumes will illustrate this idea of modernizing a design. A wedding dress worn by a student, Figure 81, and the drawing of a Spanish lady, Figure 82, show how one part of a historic garment was copied in its entirety, but worn in a different manner. The Spanish lady wears her mantilla over a high comb, but the student is wearing her mantilla over a small pill-box hat. Note, however, the extreme difference between the elaboration of the Spanish dress and shawl and the simplicity of the peau de soie dress with its matching train.

FIGURE 89*   FIGURE 90

*Reprinted with permission Alinari-Art Reference Bureau.

Figure 83 shows a student busily draping her dress form. She is experimenting with her design first in muslin before she begins with the dress fabrics. Figures 84 and 85 show her completed black crepe dress with an underblouse trimmed in off-white lace. This student was inspired by a single suggestion, the shape of the overlapped blouse. She found this idea in the painting reproduced in Figure 86, then she designed the remainder of the frock.

Figure 87 shows a drawing of a simple peasant costume of an ancient Scottish period. A modern version of the cape is seen in Figure 88. The modern design has been shaped to give semi-fitted lines and more vertical emphasis than found in the Scottish costume.

An orator of early Rome is seen in the statue shown Figure 89, whereas the sketch (Figure 90) shows a modern short formal with draped lines much like those in the Roman toga.

FIGURE 91*   FIGURE 92

* Painting by Van Dyck, Paolo Adorno, copyright The Frick Collection, New York, reprinted with permission.

FIGURE 93

FIGURE 94*

The painting by Van Dyck, Figure 91, could well have been the inspiration for the long formal gown and coat designed by Dior for Vogue, Pattern Number 1398, and sketched here, Figure 92.

The sketch shown in Figure 93 may be a modern adaptation of either Figure 94 or 95. The principal difference in converting it to today's fashions lies in the body of the fabric. In each of the two paintings the fabric is soft and filmy, whereas in the sketch the fabric seems to have more body. This change in hand is probably due to underlining, commonly used in today's fabric treatment.

*Reprinted with permission, The Metropolitan Museum of Art, Harris Brisbane Dick Fund, 1926.

FIGURE 95*

*Gerard, Pauline Borghese and Maid of Honor, California Palace of Legion of Honor, San Francisco, lent by Prince and Princess Metternich, reproduced with permission.

FIGURE 96*   FIGURE 97

Figure 96 brings the reader to this century showing a design of 1922. The sketch accompanying it, Figure 97, shows a two-piece garment popular today but with the same basic lines as the older dress. There is considerable difference in the skirt lengths between 1922 and 1967, although skirts were considered short at that time.

* Reprinted with permission from Fashion: 1965, by Mila Conti, Odyssey Press, New York, 1965.

Exercise in Adapting an Historic Design

Go to the library for books on historic design.   There are many very fine ones.   Choose one design which appeals to you.   In the space below
1. Show the sketch or tracing of the historic dress which you have chosen.   Give the complete reference.
2. Sketch an adaptation of the selected design in a garment for today.

Summary

The purpose of this unit has been to give the reader an understanding of the importance of clothing to the individual who is a member of the very complex, and often indifferent, society of today's Western world. This unit also reviews briefly the basic art background which preceded this course for the student.

Clothing appeal, the influence of the social order upon dress, the strength of fashion, and the influence of self-concept on one's clothing selection have been discussed. These four factors stress the impact of society upon the individual and have strong implications for all selection of wearing apparel.

The section on wardrobe study has been developed to help the reader consider that which she must employ in careful planning of a satisfactory wardrobe for today's type of life. This is handled in brief form, since it is review for the student.

The discussion of whether to buy or whether to make a garment should assist one in the evaluation of skills, time, and money. One should consider also the satisfactions which can be derived from this form of self-expression. If the reader has decided to make the garment, she has found suggestions on designing and making an individual garment, one which represents the wearer, her values, and her feeling for beauty. Through this garment she is presenting her image to the society in which she lives.

May the reader try, experiment, grow, and create! These experiences will give her a great sense of fulfillment, much satisfaction, and a wardrobe which can be labelled, "Mine, Exclusively!"

REFERENCES

1. Edna Meshke, *Textiles and Clothing Analysis and Synthesis*, (Minneapolis, 1961), 1.
2. Paulena Nickell and Jane Muir Dorsey, *Management in Family Living*, (New York, 1963) 21.
3. Mary Shaw Ryan, Clothing: *A Study in Human Behavior*, (New York, 1963) 2.
4. Mary Lou Rosencranz, "Social and Psychological Approach to Clothing Research," *The Journal of Home Economics*, Vol 57-1, p. 26-29.
5. Mary Shaw Ryan, *op. cit.*
6. Johnny LaRue Dorsey, "Clothing and Grooming as Related to Personality Adjustment in a Group of College Freshmen Girls," unpublished Master's Thesis, Texas Technological College, Lubbock, Texas, 1963, p. 49.
7. Paulena Nickell and Jane Muir Dorsey, *op. cit.*, p. 20.
8. Harriet T. McJimsey, Art in Clothing Selection, (New York, 1963) p. 4.
9. Norma Compton, "Motivations Underlying Clothing Selection and Wearing," 1964, Vol. 65-1, p. 40.
10. Paulena Nickell and Jan Muir Dorsey, *op. cit.*, p. 472.
11. Irene Oppenheim, *The Family as Consumers*, (New York, 1965) p. 129.

12. Mary Ellen Roach and Joanne Bubolz Eicher, *Dress, Adornment, and the Social Order,* (New York, 1965) p. 279.
13. Helen G. Chamber and Verna Moulton, *Clothing Selection,* (Chicago, 1961) p. 9.
14. Alfred Louis Kroeber, *On the Principle Order in Civilization as Exemplified by Changes of Fashion,* (Washington D. C., 1919) p. 235-263.
15. Agnes Young, *Recurring Cycles of Fashion,* (New York, 1937) p. 11-19.
16. Harriet T. McJimsey, *op. cit.,* p. 2.
17. Mildred Thurlow Tate and Oris Glisson, *Family Clothing,* (New York, 1961) p. 73.
18. Irene Oppenheim, *op. cit.,* p. 127.
19. Cecil W. Beaton, The *Glass of Fashion,* (New York, 1954) p. 381.
20. Paul Nystrom, *Economics of Fashion,* (New York, 1928) p. 3-9.
21. Mary Shaw Rayn, *op. cit.,* p. 73.
22. Emmi Cotton, *Clothes Make Magic,* (New York, 1949) p. 193.
23. Helen L. Brockman, *The Theory of Fashion Design,* (New York, 1965) p. 45.
24. Mary E. Guthrie, Viletta Leite and June Ericson, *The Arts of Costume and Personal Appearance,* (New York, 1955) p. 19.
25. Mary Shaw Ryan, *op. cit.,* p. 83.
26. Mary E. Guthrie, Vilette Leite and June Ericson, *op. cit.,* p. 4.
27. Helen G. Chanmber and Verna Moulton, *op. cit.,* p. 152-155.
28. Irene Oppenheim, *op. cit.,* p. 133.
29. Emmi Cotton, *op. cit.,* p. 193.
30. Mary E. Guthrie, Viletta Leite and June Ericson, *op. cit.,* p. 9-10.
31. Helen G. Chamber and Verna Moulton, *op. cit.,* p. 3.
32. *Ibid.,* p. 54.
33. Kay Wildham Caddel, "The Relationship between Personality Traits and Color Selection of Fabric as Found in a Group of Students," unpublished Master's thesis, Texas Technological College, Lubbock, Texas, 1966, p. 37.
34. Paulena Nickell and Jane Muir Dorsey, *op. cit.,* p. 478.
35. Helen G. Chamber and Verna Moulton, *op. cit.,* p. 4.
36. Mabel Erwin and Lila Kinchen, Clothing for Moderns, (New York, 1964) p. 585.
37. Harriet T. McJimsey, *op. cit.,* p. 112, 250.

BIBLIOGRAPHY

Anspach, Kathryn, "Clothing Selection and the Mobility Concept," *Journal of Home Economics.* 1961, Vol. 53-6, p. 438-440.

Beaton, Cecil W., *The Glass of Fashion,* (New York: Doubleday Doren and Company, 1954).

Borror, Norma J., "Relation of Physical Color and Personality Characteristics to Color Preferences to Clothes," Unpublished Master's thesis, Michigan State University, East Lansing, Michigan, 1965.

Brockman, Helen L., *The Theory of Fashion Design,* (New York: John Wiley and Sons, Inc., 1965).

Caddel, Kay Wildham, "The Relationship Between Personality Traits and Color Selection of Fabric as Found in a Group of Students," unpublished Master's thesis, Texas Technological College, Lubbock, Texas, 1966.

Chamber, Helen G. and Moulton, Verna, *Clothing Selection,* (Chicago: J. B. Lippincott Company, 1961).

Compton, Norma, "Body Image Boundries in Relation to Clothing Fabric and Design Preferences of a Group of Hospitalized Psychotic Women," *Journal of Home Economics,* Vol 56-1, p. 40-45.

Cotton, Emmi, *Clothes Make Magic,* (New York: C. P. Dalton and Company, 1949).

Erwin, Mabel and Kinchen, Lila, *Clothing for Moderns,* (New York: MacMillan Company, 1964).

Evans, S. Evelyn, "Motivations Underlying Clothing Selection and Wearing," 1964, *Journal of Home Economics,* Vol. 56-10, p. 739-743.

Fogarty, Ann, *Wife Dressing,* (New York: Julian Messener, Inc., 1959).

Goldstein, Harriett and Goldstein, Vetta, *Art in Everyday Life,* (New York: Macmillan Company, 1954).

Guthrie, Mary E. and Leite, Viletta, and Ericson, June, *Morton's The Art of Costume and Personal Appearance,* (New York: John Wiley and Sons, Inc., 1955).

Hartman, George W., "Clothing: Personal Problems and Social Issues," 1949 *Journal of Home Economics,* Vol 41-6.

Heagney, Eileen and Lyle, Dorothy Siegert and Wilbur, June, "Creative Talents in Textiles and Clothing are Encouraged by New Educational Instruments," 1966 *Journal of Home Economics,* Vol. 58-4, p. 271.

Hillhouse, Marion and Mansfield, Evelyn A., *Dress Design,* (Boston: Houghton Mifflin Company, 1948).

Hollen, Norma, *Flat Pattern Methods,* (Minneapolis: Burgess Publishing Company, 1961).

Iowa Home Economics Association, *Unit Method of Sewing,* (Ames: Iowa State University Press, 1959).

Knowles, Betty, "Factors Which Influence the Development of Good Taste In The Clothing Habits of Senior Girls," unpublished thesis, Texas Technological College, Lubbock, Texas, 1961.

Kroeber, A. L., "On The Principle Order in Civilization as Exemplified by Changes of Fashion," *American Anthropologist,* Vol 21-3, 1919).

Langner, James, *Importance of Wearing Clothes,* (New York: John Wiley and Sons, Inc., 1961).

Lockhart, Bill and Beitler, Ethel Jane, *Design For You,* (New York: John Wiley and Sons, Inc., 1961).

McInnes, Jacqueline Hobbs, "Relationship Between Color Choice and Selection Preferences of the Individual," unpublished thesis, Florida State University, Tallehassee, Florida.

McJimsey, Hariet T., *Art in Clothing Selection,* (New York: Harper and Row Publishers, 1963).

Meshke, Edna, *Textiles and Clothing Analysis and Synthesis,* (Minneapolis: Burgess Publishing Company, 1961).

Nickell, Paulena and Dorsey, Jane Muir, *Management in Family Living,* (New York: John Wiley and Sons, Inc., 1963).

Nystrom, Paul, *Economics of Fashion,* (New York: Ronald Press Company, 1928).

Oppenheim, Irene, *The Family As Consumers,* (New York: Macmillan Company, 1965).

Parnes, Sidney J. and Harding, Harold F., *A Source Book For Creative Thinking,* (New York: Charles Scribners Sons, 1962).

Pucci, Count Emilio, *Fashion,* (New York: The Odessy Press, 1965).

Roach, Mary Ellen and Eicher, Joanne Bubolz, *Dress, Adornment, and The Social Order,* (New York: John Wiley and Sons, Inc., 1965).

Rosencranz, Mary Lou, "Clothing Symbolism," 1962, *Journal of Home Economics* Vol. 54-1, p. 18-22.

Rosencranz, Mary Lou, "Social and Psychological Approach to Clothing Research" 1965, The *Journal of Home Economics,* Vol 57-1, p. 26-29.

Ryan, Mary Shaw, *Clothing: A Study in Human Behavior,* (New York: Holt, Reinhart and Winston, Inc., 1966).

Ryan, Mildred Graves and Phillips, Velma, *Clothes For You,* (New York: Appleton-Century Company, 1947).

Tate, Mildred Thurlow and Glisson, Oris, *Family Clothing,* (New York: John Wiley and Sons, Inc., 1961.

Young, Agnes, *Recurring Cycles of Fashion,* (New York: Harper and Brothers, 1937).

Appendix A

Dress Forms on the Market

Montgomery Ward and Company
Chicago, Illinois

> Silhouette Form No. 16A-64-46M; fits all sizes up to 42". (Tape)

> Slide-Hold Action Form; adjusts at six vital points.
> The following model numbers refer to sizes:

> No. 16A-64-01AK   (29 inches to 36 inches)
> No. 16A-64-02AK   (32 inches to 39 inches)
> No. 16A-64-03AK   (36 inches to 43 inches)

$19.00

Rite Dress Form Manufacturing Company   *311   N. Des Plaines St. Rm. 302*
~~3227 South Shields~~
~~Chicago, Illinois 60616~~   *Chic, Ill. 60606*

> The Rite Non-Adjustable Dress Form No. N-100 is available in
> seven sizes: 28 through 40 inch bust.

> The Rite 10 Section Adjustable Dress Form No. N-100 is avail-
> able in four sizes: 0 through 3 (30 inches to 50 inches).

> The Rite-Fit Dress Form Kit No. K-105.

Phone: 312 (454-1836)

Sears Roebuck and Company
925 South Homan
Chicago, Illinois

> Adjustable Form: No. 25A- 22281   (Sizes 32-39)
> No. 25A- 22291   (Sizes 36-43)

> Tape Kit: No. 25A- 2345C

Stewart Form, Inc.
920 Kline Street
La Jolla, California

> Made of soft plastic foam in sizes: petite, small, medium,
> medium-large, and large.

> Cover sizes to correspond with the form sizes.

Welek Fabrics
315 North 10th Street
Saint Louis 1, Missouri

> Acme Adjustable

> Acme Non-Adjustable

Appendix B

Suggested Laboratory Problems

Problems in Techniques of Draping

I. Blouses
    A. Blouse Back
    B. Blouse Fronts
        1. with underarm dart and vertical dart (one half)
        2. with shoulder dart and vertical dart (one half)
        3. with diagonal dart (one half) with lowered neckline and with
            with attached facing
        4. French dart bodice (one half - front)
        5. Design a blouse front (to be scored).
            a. with fabric supplied by instructor
            b. in muslin (whole front - to be scored)
(Two blouse half-fronts are fitted at the same time - one on each side
 of the blouse back.)

II. Skirts
    A. 1-gore (front only)
    B. 4-gore (back only)
    C. 6-gore (front only). Both #1 and #3 will be fitted with skirt back #2.
    D. Flared skirt. Drape either back or front in tissue paper.

III. Necklines and Collars
    A. Collar with low roll
    B. Collar with high roll (height determined by what is becoming to the
        wearer)
    Designed to become part of the basic pattern

IV. Sleeves
    Each student will make basic set-in sleeves by the basic flat pattern and
    fit in one blouse.

    Variations in sleeves will be done in the individual designs selected for
    garment construction.

Appendix C

Scoring Chart for Dress Forms

Check list for Scoring	Points	
	Possible	Made
Firmness	20	
Neatness	20	
Accuracy of line	20	
Handwork	20	
Total	80	

Appendix D

Scoring Chart — Draping in the Blouse Area

Check List for Scoring	Points	
	Possible	Made
Over-all Appearance	20	
Grainline Direction	10	
Darts	10	
Ease	10	
Shoulder - Line Armseye -	10	
Seam allowance	10	
Neckline	10	
Interpretation of Design	10	
Total	90	